HERE TO STAY

HERE TO STAY

THE STORY OF THE CLASS OF WOMEN WHO COEDUCATED THE UNIVERSITY OF VIRGINIA

GAIL BURRELL GERRY

UNIVERSITY OF VIRGINIA PRESS
Charlottesville and London

The University of Virginia Press is situated on the traditional lands of the Monacan Nation, and the Commonwealth of Virginia was and is home to many other Indigenous people. We pay our respect to all of them, past and present. We also honor the enslaved African and African American people who built the University of Virginia, and we recognize their descendants. We commit to fostering voices from these communities through our publications and to deepening our collective understanding of their histories and contributions.

University of Virginia Press
© 2025 by the Rector and Visitors of the University of Virginia
All rights reserved
Printed in the United States of America on acid-free paper

First published 2025

1 3 5 7 9 8 6 4 2

LIBRARY OF CONGRESS CATALOGING-IN-PUBLICATION DATA

Names: Gerry, Gail B., author.
Title: Here to stay : the story of the class of women who coeducated the University of Virginia / Gail Burrell Gerry.
Description: Charlottesville : University of Virginia Press, 2025. | Includes bibliographical references and index.
Identifiers: LCCN 2024045105 (print) | LCCN 2024045106 (ebook) | ISBN 9780813952819 (hardcover) | ISBN 9780813952826 (paperback) | ISBN 9780813952833 (ebook)
Subjects: LCSH: University of Virginia—History. | Coeducation—Virginia—Charlottesville—History. | Women college students—Virginia—Charlottesville—History. | Women college students—Virginia—Charlottesville—Social conditions. | Single-sex schools—Virginia—Charlottesville—History.
Classification: LCC LD5678 .G47 2025 (print) | LCC LD5678 (ebook) | DDC 378.1/9820755481—dc23/eng/20241031
LC record available at https://lccn.loc.gov/2024045105
LC ebook record available at https://lccn.loc.gov/2024045106

Illustrations courtesy of the Albert and Shirley Small Special Collections Library, University of Virginia, unless otherwise noted

Cover photo: Scott Stadium, September 1970, author on right. (Albert and Shirley Small Special Collections Library, University of Virginia)
Cover design: Cecilia Sorochin

*To the women who began their undergraduate studies in the College of
Arts and Sciences at the University of Virginia on September 18, 1970,*

*and to all the women at UVA who came before
us and on whose shoulders we stood,*

*and to Larry, Alison, and Lisa, who became research assistants,
editors, and all-around supporters of this book*

The past is never dead. It's not even past.
—William Faulkner

CONTENTS

FOREWORD BY TERESA A. SULLIVAN   xi

Prologue   1

1. Changing Times   11

2. UVA's Journey to Coeducation   22

3. The First Cadre of Women   53

4. By God, I Think They're Here . . .   70

5. . . . To Stay   101

6. Trailblazers and Pioneers   128

7. The World We're Living Into   151

Epilogue   167

AFTERWORD BY CARLA WILLIAMS   177
ACKNOWLEDGMENTS   181
CHRONOLOGY   183
NOTES   187
BIBLIOGRAPHY   193
INDEX   201

FOREWORD

A lot was happening in the summer of 1970. The invasion of Cambodia, the aftermath of killings at Kent State and Jackson State, demonstrated opposition to the Vietnam War, and civil rights activism rocked the country and the country's universities. In the noise and confusion, a quiet revolution was coming to pass at the University of Virginia. For the first time, a large cohort of women was admitted as first-year students to the College of Arts and Sciences. Many of them would go on to become graduates in the class of 1974. Gail Burrell Gerry, who was one of those young women, has compiled new research, including interviews, to chronicle her classmates' experiences as they approached their golden anniversary as alumnae.

By 1970 coeducation was no longer big national news. The Ivy League had admitted women during the preceding decade; most private universities had done so far earlier. Most public institutions had been born coeducational, and for those that were not, the University of Virginia and military institutions were the principal holdouts. Within Virginia, William & Mary and Virginia Tech were already coed. And even at Virginia, as Gerry carefully documents, women had been admitted to graduate and professional schools. Women could transfer as third- and fourth-year students into education and nursing, and some faculty daughters and wives and eventually some women residents of Charlottesville were allowed to matriculate. The quiet revolution of 1970 was the admission of a large cohort of first-year women to the College of Arts and Sciences.

Although coeducation had been discussed for years, and various committees and task forces had studied it, in the end it took a federal lawsuit filed by the ACLU, the enterprise of a young lawyer named John Lowe, and the courage of named plaintiff Virginia Scott to shatter the inertia. The university enlarged the next entering class so that no qualified male applicants would be excluded but so that a large number of female applicants would also be admitted. These women were carefully vetted. Grades, test scores, and recommendations were not enough; they were also judged for the intangible "grit" that was thought essential to their success.

Full coeducation posed some obstacles in terms of physical capital such as residence halls, gym facilities, and restrooms in classroom buildings. To the administrators' credit, these obstacles were addressed. The issue of adequate lighting for nighttime safety would not be fully addressed for many years, and it is still a challenge for women students living off-Grounds. Far more consequential in many ways, however, were the cultural and social obstacles of resistance by alumni, some faculty, and many male students. The resistance was by no means uniform, however, and after a half-century of reflection many of the women graduates recall their college days with affection and nostalgia.

Gerry traces the impressive careers and leadership of this pioneering group of women graduates, often using their own words. As graduates, they touched nearly every sector of enterprise, pursuing careers in law, medicine, entertainment, education, and management. A visit to Grounds today reveals women students who are Olympians, Rhodes Scholars, Distinguished Majors, and leaders of all sorts. UVA alumnae are found today in the U.S. Senate and the House of Representatives, state legislatures, the U.S. Foreign Service, the federal judiciary, CEO suites, healthcare organizations large and small, and leadership positions in business, industry, and nonprofits. They are university professors and small business owners, ministers and rabbis. Many if not most of them are active citizens and voters. And to the great benefit of their families, they are wives, mothers, and grandmothers, and some of them are now in the UVA parent body with their own students on Grounds.

Gail Burrell Gerry has told a hopeful story of how the new entrants in fall of 1970 led to a long-term future in which UVA includes people of all types from the Commonwealth and beyond. Coeducation has enriched the academic and social climate of UVA. Social change can be messy and uncomfortable, and despite this, the long-term effects of this social change have greatly benefited the class of 1974, their successors, the university, and the Commonwealth of Virginia.

Teresa A. Sullivan
President Emerita and University Professor
University of Virginia

HERE TO STAY

PROLOGUE

If you didn't see it coming, you weren't paying attention.

A LTHOUGH I'VE NEVER EXPERIENCED one, I've heard others describe a flashback, the feeling of reliving an event or even a moment—sometimes good, sometimes harrowing. While researching and writing this book, though, I did begin to dream more about my college years at the University of Virginia. As a member of the first class of undergraduate women in 1970, I reconnected with former classmates and listened to their accounts from the past. As I did, I experienced more anxiety dreams or, more accurately, nightmares.[1] Recurring was the one where I'm racing up and down stairs, through dark hallways trying to locate a classroom—in my case, a math class—knowing I would arrive too late to take the final exam and, as a result, would not graduate with my class.

But more often during this process, I had moments of déjà vu. It actually started before I thought about writing this book, with the run-up to the 2016 presidential elections, and grew more persistent in the following years. I would find myself in the uncomfortable position of feeling like I had already lived through an experience. When women were publicly and openly called inappropriate and vile names, it gave me pause. Haven't I experienced this before? When women's looks and dress were a topic of public discussion and sometimes ridicule, it conjured up vivid memories. Hadn't we worked hard to get beyond this? When equal pay and a woman's right to have control over her own body continued to be litigated, I felt in my bones the battles we'd fought decades ago.

I worked for more than forty years as an educator and researcher, and during my career, I facilitated hundreds of planning and other work groups. Often, I would start new groups with the icebreaker, "What would you tell your eighteen-year-old self?"[2] Without fail, contemplating this question and sharing the roads they had traveled since this pivotal birthday moved some participants to tears. It's the birthday many consider the coming of age. Turning eighteen is deemed a rite of passage into adulthood both legally and, often, physically and emotionally. What is so compelling about this exercise is that this birthday typically happens right around high school graduation, a time when we are making important decisions—decisions that shape the rest of our lives.

For many of us, these decisions included where we would attend college. Not if. That decision had been made by us, our parents, or other family members much earlier in our lives. But the "where" was the critical question and, ultimately, decision. In his book *The Years That Matter Most: How College Makes or Breaks Us*, Paul Tough suggests that this decision is a pivotal one, especially as it relates to social and economic class mobility. Tough states, "Mobility in the United States today depends, in large part, on what happens to individuals during a relatively brief period in late adolescence and early adulthood." He continues, "The decisions you make about higher education—and the decisions that are made for you—play a critical role in determining the course of the rest of your life."[3]

Now, decades later, I view things differently than I did when I was a young person of eighteen. Today, I look back on some of the situations, experiences, and relationships in a different light than when I was fully immersed in them. Time and distance change perspectives. Some things that were incredibly important and that felt "huge" when I was eighteen are of little significance many years later. And things I didn't give a second thought when I was young I now realize were of great importance. They shaped my life journey. To that point, I didn't realize what it would mean to be one of the women who entered UVA in the late summer of 1970, but over the years its impact has endured.

In 2020, with the fiftieth anniversary of our arrival at UVA in 1970, there was renewed interest in our class. It prompted a *Virginia Magazine* "special anniversary issue" and an online summit, entitled ReTold, coordinated by UVA's Alumni Association in collaboration with UVA's Maxine Platzer Lynn Women's Center.[4] But still, there are aspects of the university's coeducation journey that haven't been told. When pitching the idea of this book to the University of Virginia Press, I emphasized that its significance would be in the telling of the human side of UVA's coeducation journey.

Until now, the exploration of the culture and traditions of the university during the years prior to women entering the freshman class, and during the four years women matriculated and graduated, has only scratched the surface. There have been occasional articles, symposia, and exhibits, but nowhere has the story of the first class of women been told in depth. Uplifting these women's voices is particularly meaningful because they forged new ground in an institution that advertised itself as, and took great pride in being, a school for "Virginia gentlemen."[5]

There is power in hearing the firsthand accounts of those who participated in UVA's transformation. And though I am part of it, this is not solely my story. This story is of all the women, 367 strong, who started as freshmen—or "first-years," in University of Virginia–speak—in the late summer of 1970, the first year of undergraduate coeducation at the University of Virginia.[6] It is about our experiences then, and our experiences after. This book explores the stories of my fellow classmates—what we faced as we prepared for college, what we recall about our first days and months at UVA, and what the journey was like until graduation, which for most of us was May 19, 1974. We looked back, now fifty-plus years later, to describe what—and how much—being in the pioneering class of women at UVA contributed to making us the women we are today.

Even while revisiting the conflicts and controversies of the late 1960s and early 1970s, writing this book reminded me of the pure joy of being young. Of seeing and experiencing the world through youthful eyes. Many of my classmates and I were unfamiliar with the University of Virginia and the city of Charlottesville, and the glory of our surroundings came as a sweet surprise. We marveled at the beauty of the Grounds, the term UVA students, faculty, and alumni use for "campus," and we explored different paths to class through gardens and by pavilions. As late summer turned to fall during our first semester, the leaves changed, and we began to get our bearings. We found classmates with cars who drove us to the mountains or surrounding countryside. The first snowfall brought a bit of magic to walking the Lawn, a large grassy area on campus surrounded by residential and academic buildings. As dusk fell, and with snow enveloping us, it felt like we were in our own private cocoon. And who isn't enchanted by a Virginia spring? One day it's gray and cold; the next, the sky is brilliant blue, and trees we never noticed are covered with colorful blooms.

As I read my classmates' responses to the online open-ended survey that I distributed, I found myself smiling and reliving happy memories. Memories of friendships and academic debates. Stories of taking a class that piqued an interest in a subject that would later turn into a passion and a rewarding career. Gaining the confidence to speak up for a point of view that might not be popular but that we felt strongly about. Meeting a special person with whom we might commit to share a life, even if it sometimes was more short-term than expected.

This project permitted me to reflect in a way that I hadn't before. And by sharing our stories and comparing notes, I was able to see the resonance in my and my fellow classmates' experiences at UVA, how being part of the group of women to coeducate the university impacted us then and reverberates in our lives since. Something I heard again and again was that while it wasn't easy, our college experiences served as preparation for the journeys that awaited us postgraduation. Many of us went on to work in fields with few to no other women. We were part of the first generation in the United States where the vast majority of women worked, including most women with children. The world was changing, and our arrival on Grounds was part of that. We were forging new ground, and as it turned out for many of us, it wouldn't be the last time.

Now, fast-forward to today, we're in late midlife, which can be both challenging and rewarding. There are new physical realities and sometimes limitations. After decades of work and often demanding careers, many of us are finding our place in a world that doesn't include daily paid employment. If we have children, they are adults now, many with families of their own. We have new blocks of uninterrupted time that our earlier busyness precluded. There is time for reflection. Time to really live the life that we said we wanted to live. Putting our family first, not only in thoughts and words, but in actual time and energy. Using our "best hours" to do the things that we believe are most important in creating the legacy we want to leave.

Gathering Stories

In her book *The Education of an Idealist: A Memoir*, Samantha Power said, "We make sense of our lives through stories. Regardless of our different backgrounds and perspectives, stories bind us."[7] I've used a variety of sources to tell this story, the story of the women who at seventeen and eighteen years of age arrived in Charlottesville as part of an academic and social transformation. I contacted every female classmate I could find. During the years 2019 to 2024, I sent online interviews to most, phoned others, and met in person with some. The stories of the women who entered in September 1970 are the backbone of this book. I feel truly privileged to have been let into the lives of dozens of women who shared personal, sometimes private, and often inspiring parts of their life story with me. Some of these stories are hard and troubling. And some of the information suggests a different, more nuanced way of looking at this important part of UVA's history.

Larry Sabato (Arts and Sciences, '74), who was president of the student council our fourth year and is the founder and director of UVA's Center for Politics, spoke about some people's hesitancy to share tough stories. He said he knew from talking with women from our class that some had stories they would never tell. He made the analogy to his own father, who, despite Larry's urging, wouldn't tell him about his World War II experiences. Larry recounted it wasn't until after his father's death and his discovery of a scrapbook his father kept that he would know his father's wartime story. While for most of us, our time at UVA felt nothing like going to war, it is true that for many of us, it was at times challenging, trying, and, for some, traumatic. During our four years, a lot happened to each of us individually and to all of us collectively, and we can hold these experiences and truths together.

A difficult part of writing this book was not being able to include all the stories I heard and read. And what woke me in the middle of the night was knowing there were stories I still don't know. In some cases, I reached out to women whose perspective I was told needed to be included. Others reached out to me. And, of course, there were some women in our class with whom I was never able to connect, despite great effort.

In addition to my female classmates, I spoke with male students in our class, former students in classes that preceded us, and current and former administrators and professors. I participated in webinars, listened to podcasts, and read transcripts of oral histories. The quotes and comments included in the text are from first-person interviews, conversations, and communications unless the source is otherwise noted. I also examined multiple accounts and sources that spanned more than fifty years, including a survey of fifty women conducted in 1971 by the Office of Student Affairs and analyzed by E. A. Mayer for her UVA doctoral dissertation, and a second survey that was conducted fourteen years later of twenty-eight of the same women for Louise Lilley Robertson's doctoral dissertation at the College of William and Mary.[8] There were surveys conducted about living on the Lawn and a survey sent to alumnae under President John Casteen's name in 1998 (he served as UVA's president from 1990 to 2010), and the basis of a seminal article by Phyllis Leffler, history professor emerita. I read books and articles, seven years of the *Cavalier Daily* (the UVA student newspaper), and memos from and accountings by former administrators. The data were messy and the story complex. Not everyone agreed on everything.

Along the way, there were surprises and frustrations. For example, no one at UVA could provide the exact enrollment numbers for that first class of women admitted to the college. No one knew for sure how many Black women entered in 1970, nor how many graduated. It was perplexing to me that a court-sanctioned coeducation plan required so little documentation. As a researcher who would rely on evidence for reports I wrote, this was unfamiliar territory. Suggestions to use the *Cavalier Daily* and *Charlottesville Daily Progress* articles that contained demographic and enrollment information, or UVA's yearbook, *Corks and Curls*, or commencement programs, while seemingly helpful, are most likely what has caused the prevailing confusion and misinformation about the composition of our class in 1970. After weeks in the archives, I found the official enrollment document, Dean of Admissions Ernest (Ernie) Ern's report to the State Council of Higher Education for Virginia (SCHEV). The document helped clarify the question of how many women started in 1970. But it didn't answer the question of how many of us stayed.

The Ern report indicated that women comprised 18 percent of the College of Arts and Sciences' class of 1974, not 39.5 percent, which had been previously reported.[9] This official number helps make sense of the anecdotal information I was gathering from women in the class. I heard from numerous women that they were often the only woman, or one of two women, in a class.

Challenging Times

The timeframe for writing and publishing this book (2019 to 2024) traversed one of the most difficult periods in our country's history—a global pandemic that over the course of three years would claim the lives of more than one million Americans and seven million people worldwide.[10] Life changed in a matter of weeks to one of isolation, closed public facilities, and serious health fears. This was especially true, at least initially, for people the ages of my classmates and me. While I tried to soldier on, like all my friends and neighbors, many typical book-writing tasks couldn't happen. UVA's archives, the critical source of the facts and historical backstories of UVA's coeducation process, initially closed, then limited access to students and faculty. Timelines shifted and work got done, just on a different schedule and in different circumstances. Fortunately, this story has a long shelf life. Institutional transformation is as relevant today as it was fifty-plus years ago.

And, during the editing of this manuscript, one of the saddest events in the University of Virginia's history occurred—the November 13, 2022, shooting deaths of three student athletes and the wounding of another student athlete and student in a parking garage on Grounds.[11] The shooter was reported to be another student. The tragic loss of three vibrant, accomplished young men—Devin Chandler, Lavel Davis Jr., and D'Sean

Perry—shocked and saddened the UVA community. The public grief belied private soul searching about the culture of guns and violence that is unfortunately but indisputably part of schools, campus life, and American society, writ large.

This book focuses on the first class of women to matriculate at the College of Arts and Sciences, but it is important to note that the university was undergoing another cultural change during the early 1970s, with increased admission and recruitment of Black students. Maurice Apprey, a professor at UVA and coeditor of *The Key to the Door*, a book recounting the stories of some of the first Black students at UVA, speaks to the dissonance he sometimes feels about his fondness for UVA, the place where he works and calls home, and the stories of pain and isolation he heard from pioneering Black students. In the preface to his book, he speaks of the young Black men who were forced to seek their education elsewhere as well as the brave few who took their place in classes where they were clearly not welcome.[12]

Apprey writes, "We cannot easily make amends to those African Americans whose educations elsewhere was paid by the state. Nor can we erase the unnecessarily cruel treatment that those who attended the University at that time experienced."

My Biases

One classmate, before agreeing to an interview, wanted to know my "slant" for this book. I explained that I didn't have one, that my plan was to see where the stories of my fellow classmates, as well as those of other key players, took me. In retrospect, I could have quoted UVA's founder, President Thomas Jefferson, saying I would be "bold in the pursuit of knowledge, never fearing to follow truth and reason to whatever results they led," but that seemed a bit lofty, even if apropos. The truth is, I didn't have an angle except to acknowledge that our collective story is complex. And the more I read and reread interview transcripts and online responses from my classmates, the more I believe that. Through years of research and conversations, in person, online, and by phone, I stayed committed to the story that emerged, the story in this book.

During my professional career, I was often in the role of participant observer, as I am as author of this book. In this role, I believe it is critical to be transparent, and where there are biases, to name them. In that spirit, I must state that I am a proud University of Virginia alumna. I have wonderful memories of my years on Grounds, and I received an excellent education. I have dear friends of more than fifty years because of my attendance at UVA. I met my husband, also an alum, my first year, his second, and we married the day before I graduated. Our older daughter is an alumna. It was my love for the university that prompted my examination of its history and traditions and my desire to view it through the lens of the pioneering women who, in one year, changed its face and its future. I took on the telling of this story with a tremendous curiosity and openness about what I would discover.

The Book's Title

The title of this book comes from one of the most iconic *Cavalier Daily* articles written during UVA's coeducation journey. Steve Grimwood's "By God, I Think They're Here to Stay" was the third-page headline in the inaugural issue of the student newspaper that "welcomed" us on September 14,

The women who entered in 1970 were "welcomed" by this article. (*Cavalier Daily*, September 14, 1970)

1970, the first day of official events during our orientation.[13] It has been reprinted repeatedly. Rebecca (Bek) Sorrells Wheeler, shown lugging her suitcases to her suite in Webb, smiling in a self-made velveteen miniskirt, has been memorialized in that moment for more than half of a century. In his coeducation story, Grimwood quoted a high school principal in Mississippi—the state that actively resisted *Brown v. Board of Education* the longest—from remarks he made about finally opening formerly all-white public-school doors to Black students in January 1970.

Grimwood wrote, "Some superb male chauvinists on the grounds have likened our situation to that of the South, namely forced (sexual) integration under the directive of a court order. But no matter what your opinion may be, remember the words of Elmer O. Jaffe, principal of Columbia High, Columbia, Miss., 'By God, I think they are here to stay.'"[14]

ONE

CHANGING TIMES

Youth is wasted on the young.
—George Bernard Shaw

A S A MEMBER OF the first class of women at the University of Virginia, I vividly remember one of my first public encounters with a male student who disdained the changes that were occurring. It was in a public speaking class my first year. I listened as he, a second-year student, gave a speech about what was lost when UVA admitted my class of women. He sported a large button on his sports coat lapel that read, "BBTOU," which we all knew stood for "Bring Back the Old U." He railed against all the change that he and, he claimed, many other men thought was destroying what was special about *their* university. As I sat there, my face burning, I hatched a plan to counter the speech with a parody of a woman attending the university "to find a man." The following week I delivered the speech in hot pants and glistening lip gloss, confronting his blatant sexism with, I hoped, humor. My goal was to point out the fallacy of thinking that anyone, including—and perhaps, especially—those wearing BBTOU pins, could stop progress. I am not sure I would approach my response the same way today, and not only because I would rather die than put on a pair of hot pants. Now I can no longer respond to sexism with humor.

More than fifty years later, I would read letters from alumni, solicited and received in 1968 by the Special Committee on the Admission of Women to the College, that contained the same sentiments my male classmate espoused. Multiple alumni wrote that the only reason women wanted to attend UVA was to "get a husband." Some letters said that the only good that could come from coeducation, should that happen, would be that it would make it easier and less time consuming for men to find dates.

Throughout my career as an educator and researcher, I examined institutional policies and practices predicated on deeply held beliefs and values. It never ceased to amaze me how difficult change was and continues to be. After all, institutions are merely people joined together organizationally, and people change all the time. It seems like progress should occur more easily and more rapidly.

With regard to change, the University of Virginia occupies an interesting historical position, as it was the last public university in the nation to coeducate its undergraduate programs, military institutions excepted.[1]

When I made the decision to attend the college, I was unaware of the strong sense of history and traditions going back to its founding and founder, the tradition of male chivalry and honor, and the vestiges of racism and sexism that likely kept UVA male and white long after other schools were not. Some in our first-year class, including me, were largely oblivious to what this tradition would mean to some of the male students, faculty, and alumni, and ultimately what it would mean to us.

Summer of '69

On the eve of my own adulthood, the country itself was ushering in a new era. As Bob Dylan sang, "the times they are a-changin'."[2] And boy, were they. During the 1960s and 1970s, there felt like an urgency in how young people were reckoning with the way things were, and how they thought they should be. It was an era of upheaval that saw the civil rights movement, the Vietnam War, and the women's movement, among others.

I was seventeen years old in the summer of 1969, a time in the United States that is storied for good reason. In a span of a few months, an astounding amount of history was made. Neil Armstrong and Buzz Aldrin took the first steps on the moon, and nearly four hundred thousand people converged on a dairy farm in Bethel, New York, for the Woodstock Music and Arts Festival, among them, unbeknownst to me, my future UVA boyfriend and now husband, Lawrence (Larry) Gerry. Young people around the country united to protest the war in Vietnam, a war that many believed was a mistake from the start. The world was rocked by the Manson murders, racial unrest, and the riots at the Stonewall Inn between gay rights activists and police.

During that time, I was grappling with what my life would be like after high school. As I prepared for my senior year and a college future, I was in good—and robust—company. In fact, I was one of millions of seventeen- and eighteen-year-olds all over the country. Kids in my generation would years later be labeled "baby boomers," or "boomers" for short. We already knew that there were a lot of us—we had crowded the elementary schools, junior highs, and high schools, forced the creation of more little league teams and ballet classes, and made our presence known by our sheer numbers. The question of how to accommodate our ranks made applying to college even more competitive.

I was anxious to attend college far from Ypsilanti, Michigan, the small city outside Ann Arbor where I was born and raised. I was the second oldest, the first daughter of seven children. My dad was a leader in our community and ran our family-owned cement business, A.J. Burrell and Sons. Being one of "the Burrell kids" meant something in Ypsi. I was expected to achieve excellence, and I did my best to oblige. I sang in the church choir and worked part-time at the neighborhood pharmacy. I was student council president, a Girl Scout, a cheerleader, and a synchronized swimmer. I volunteered, studied hard, read voraciously, helped with my younger siblings, and did what I could to make my family proud. In a year's time, though, unbeknownst to me then, I would go from eager learner and achiever to one of approximately 367 women who fit similar profiles and were part of the first class of undergraduates to include women at UVA.

Many of my friends would attend Eastern Michigan University, right up the street from our high school, or travel the seven miles to the University of Michigan in Ann Arbor. For me, I was eager to leave the responsibility of my home and high school behind. A new idea was planted during my junior year in high school when my family traveled to Georgia to watch my older brother play baseball with his college team. We left on a cold, windy Michigan afternoon; when we arrived at the ballfield, it was bright, sunny, and springlike. I remember sitting in the stands and marveling at the fun the home team's fans were having—music blared, young men were throwing frisbees along the baseline in the outfield, and the sky was blue. After eighteen years of frigid northern winters, I decided right then to apply to schools in the South. I chose one in-state fallback, but the rest of the schools I applied to were out-of-state, including the University of Virginia.

In the early winter of 1970, I received a letter from Mary Washington College offering me admission to their undergraduate program for the coming year. I found this odd, since I had not applied to Mary Washington College. When I met with my counselor the following morning, we discovered that I received that letter because I had applied to the University of Virginia, and Mary Washington College was the women's college for UVA. To our surprise, the University of Virginia at Charlottesville did not accept female undergraduate students. At least not yet.[3]

A mistake like this might seem strange today, but remember, we were using paper copies of college catalogs, discerning fine print to make important decisions, and sending applications via U.S. mail. The internet was a long way away. And Virginia was a long way from Michigan. In addition, not many students in my high school went to out-of-state colleges, and fewer went to the competitive southern schools to which I'd applied. It wasn't because my classmates weren't smart—they were. It was because of what I have since learned, as a former high school principal and career educator, is the tyranny of low expectations. While the Advanced Placement (AP) program began in 1955, Ypsilanti High School did not offer AP classes. They did not offer test prep sessions. It never occurred to any of us to take our SATs or ACTs multiple times to try to raise our scores. It was enough to ask our parents to pay for these admission exams once.

So, it wasn't surprising that my counselor missed the fine print and encouraged me to apply to UVA. And when shortly after receiving the acceptance to Mary Washington College, I received another letter, this time offering me admission to the University of Virginia at Charlottesville, I didn't think too much about it. Being a non-Virginian, I had no idea about the events that had been transpiring at UVA. I knew nothing of the mandate to explore coeducation, the appointment of a committee to make recommendations, nor the lawsuit that would ultimately push the Board of Visitors to accept a sizable cohort of women as undergraduates, most of whom were members of the class of 1974.

A Society in Flux

Regardless of whether you supported or resisted the changes, no one could deny that during the 1960s, American society was evolving at an incredible pace. The youth of the nation banded together in ways never seen before to raise awareness, to fight for civil rights, to call for an end of the Vietnam War, and to advance the struggle for women to enter all aspects of society. Civil and women's rights protests, along with scenes of carnage from Vietnam, were broadcasted on the evening news, beaming from black-and-white televisions across the nation.

Some historians believe that more cultural changes occurred during the 1960s than in any other time in our country's history. Coeducation of all-male universities was likely accelerated by the social changes occurring in the 1960s and was emblematic of the times. When examining the movement to coeducate UVA and other private and public universities during the 1960s, the larger societal environment must be considered.

It should also be noted that with the rise of feminism and the championing of the Equal Rights Amendment (which to this day has still not become law despite ratification by two-thirds of the states), a vocal and powerful anti-feminist movement was launched by Phyllis Schlafly and others.[4] Though Schlafly was not involved in UVA's coeducation process, she did voice strong opposition to the coeducation of Virginia Military Institute in 1996. In an open letter to VMI alumni, she stated that the effort was "a no-holds-barred fight to feminize VMI waged by the radical feminists and their cohorts in the Federal Government."[5]

The Stars Align for Coeducation

Nancy Weiss Malkiel, author of *"Keep the Damned Women Out,"* a book about coeducation at Princeton and other Ivy League colleges and universities and the parallel coeducation campaign in England, cites four distinct yet overlapping movements that set in motion the increasing call for change. The anti-war movement, the civil rights movement, the women's movement, and the student movement all combined to create a sense of urgency around cultural changes and opportunities.

The push in the 1960s to coeducate all-male colleges and universities wasn't the first time that women raised the issue of attending classes alongside men. In fact, several of the nation's most prestigious schools were founded as all-male schools. In the 1800s and early 1900s, women's rights movements often addressed coeducation as necessary to ensure that women, who were educating the youth of the nation, received a quality education themselves. In 1920, the League of Women Voters prepared a prominent plank around educational opportunities for women.

The coeducation debate would continue throughout the following decades. College administrators and trustees attempted to address the issue, in many cases, with coordinate colleges. The coordinate colleges were founded, either on or in the proximity of the main all-male campus. In other cases, graduate and professional schools were open to women, especially colleges of education or nursing. But by the 1960s, pressure was mounting for all-male colleges to admit women. Societal norms were changing, and in many cases, both men and women wanted their post–high school experience to reflect a more typical slice of the life they would lead beyond college.

As the Civil Rights Act was tested in labor and other areas of American society, there was a question about its application to postsecondary education as well. And as the last K–12 resisters to *Brown v. Board of Education* were desegregating, attention was focused on some of the male-only colleges and universities.

Yale and Princeton Go Coed

Yale and Princeton universities both went coed in 1969, and compared to other schools that were coeducating around the same time, there appears to be more archival data on their transitions. The geneses for coeducation at both Yale and Princeton have also been documented in several books. In her book *Yale Needs Women*, Anne Gardiner Perkins wrote that at that university, the male students' unrelenting insistence on coeducation positioned the president at the time against the groundswell to admit women.[6] Lanny Davis, chairman of the *Yale Daily News*, wrote in his January 26, 1966, debut editorial, "coeducation should now be beyond argument." He would go on to write eighteen pro-coeducation columns and editorials in the following five months.

Kingman Brewster Jr., in his fifth year as Yale's president, was convinced of the need to coeducate only when there was a "loss of first-rate students," that is, male students, specifically, who turned down Yale to attend colleges with "coeducational attractions."[7] He reportedly stated to alumni, "Our concern is not so much what Yale can do for women but what can women do for Yale."[8] He saw women as an attraction that would strengthen Yale's recruiting portfolio.

Princeton and other Ivy League schools were experiencing a downturn in applications as well. This, coupled with the fact that an increasing percentage of the men accepted were choosing to go elsewhere, created concerns. At Princeton, admissions officers were tasked with figuring out why such a prestigious school was not enrolling some of the finest candidates. What did men want that Princeton couldn't provide? It turned out the answer to that question was often—female students. As elite schools went coed, it sent a message that all-male status and "academic prestige" were not enough to attract top students.

While it was in Yale's self-interest to accept women, there was still some resistance to the move, especially among alumni. Letters at the time from alumni indicate their concern regarding the influence that coeducation might have on the university's culture and traditions. Some alumni even indicated that they would withhold new contributions or cancel pledges if the university moved forward with admitting women. Yale and Princeton both accepted their first class of undergraduate women in addition to the number of men accepted, increasing their enrollment, which was a strategy also employed by UVA.

As schools went coed, school culture was redefined, to varying extents. At Princeton, 200 women were admitted into the first class; at Yale, 195 women were admitted. Often, women arrived to find there wasn't a place for them in the fabric of the school community. Malkiel writes that the first class of women at Princeton found little acceptance in clubs and other organizations.[9] One woman stated that she left in the spring as she had arrived in the fall—an outsider. If anything had changed, Malkiel said, it was the women, not Princeton. Another female student suggested that her undergraduate experience was similar to her year as a foreign exchange student. She said, "I had never before felt so alone as a girl."

At Yale, women were often asked in classes, where they were vastly outnumbered by men, to "give the women's point of view." This, as one might expect, quickly became tiresome and annoying.

The term "coed," coined in the 1800s, was used to describe women who arrived at once all-male schools. Even when all-female schools admitted men later in the 1970s, it was still the women who were the coeds. Even though the "co" implies a relationship of joint involvement, "coed" is defined as a "young woman being educated at the same institution as young men." The implication was that the school belonged to the men and women were allowed entrance into their domain. At both Yale and Princeton, a powerful tradition of male camaraderie made the first years for women difficult.

Coeducating a school is not a terribly difficult academic task, although the next chapter relates that for UVA, it wasn't without challenges. But, according to the reports of women who entered in the first year of coeducation at a number of colleges and universities, the more difficult aspect of coeducating an institution is the acceptance of women as equals into the school community. Former Ukrainian ambassador Marie Yovanovitch writes that when starting her college career at Princeton in September 1976, "the Princeton community was still debating the wisdom of the decision to go coed." Her European history professor, Jerome Blum, in a discussion group where Yovanovitch was the only female, "declared that he had not been in favor of admitting women to Princeton."[10]

The coeducation journeys at Princeton and Yale would be studied and considered by the key players in UVA's path to coeducation. Because admission requirements at UVA were similar to those at Ivy League schools, and UVA would often accept students who were also accepted at an Ivy League college, UVA leadership considered Ivies as peer institutions. Ernest (Ernie) Ern, the former vice president of student affairs at

UVA who served as the dean of admissions from 1967 to 1973, recounts attending a summer session at Harvard in the late 1960s to learn more about the admissions process. Communication between and among UVA administrators and their Ivy League brothers appears to be quite common during this period. And, it seems, as goes an Ivy, often, went UVA. The timing of coeducation would be no exception, although UVA's route would be quite different.

In her book *In the Company of Educated Women*, Barbara Miller Solomon writes, "Educators at men's colleges, already concerned with rising costs and declining applicant pools, acknowledged their students' preference to have women enrolled with them. Reluctantly, in the early seventies, resistant colleges like the University of Virginia, Yale, and Princeton gave up the battle and admitted women."[11]

The Last Public University to Admit Women

Over the years, I have shared with friends, coworkers, clients, and even strangers who see me shopping, running errands, or working out in a UVA T-shirt that I was a member of the first class of women. Somehow, this felt like an important part of who I am. It described my life's journey as a pioneer and change agent. I sometimes conflated "first" with winning, and recently I have done a great deal of self-examination about my use of this word. When Yale went coed in 1969, *The New York Times* labeled the first class of women "superwomen."[12] There is something rather heady in a label like that. And exciting. Joining with a cadre of young, smart, and, yes, tough women pushing back against the patriarchy and the barrier of maleness.

Today, I am much more troubled that UVA was the *last* public university, except for military academies, to coeducate, and that being all male was not only accepted but an integral part of what made the University of Virginia the school it was. And, to some extent, still is. I have always been very proud to have been in the class of women that coeducated UVA, but only recently did it occur to me to explore and acknowledge that it took until 1970 for that to happen—and not until the university's leadership was sued.

This brings me to the critical difference in the story of coeducation at Yale and at UVA. At Yale, the movement to full coeducation, not just a token number of women undergraduates, came from within. It was the male students who rebelled against what they saw as genuine discrimination and unfairness, which was that the opportunity to access a Yale education was only possible if you were male.[13] At UVA, although the Board of Visitors (BOV) had tasked the university president to examine "whether there is a need for the admission of women to the College of Arts and Sciences at Charlottesville," and by 1969, the student council had reversed positions and strongly supported coeducation, it took a lawsuit to convince them that a male-only university was not sustainable.[14] Nor legal.

One of the reasons given by alumni for opposing the admission of women was the idea of tradition. UVA holds rich traditions handed down from the time of Thomas Jefferson—the tradition of the Virginia Gentleman, the coat and tie, the honor system, an all-male institution, the secret student societies. The exclusivity of it all. Saul Levine, professor emeritus at the University of California at San Diego, writes that traditions bring predictability and constancy to our lives, along with a sense of belonging to a group.[15] Religious and cultural traditions fulfill important criteria for achieving our sense of affiliation and community. Many older alumni and faculty, along with some students, clung tenaciously to those traditions, and women were considered unwanted interlopers in the club.

The ethical issues of affording a UVA education to only males would continue to be litigated long after women were a presence on the Grounds. What I also know now is that the first year of coeducation at UVA was described in various articles as an "experiment," implying that it might not work and might not last.

Many scholars point to coeducation as a turning point in the history of the University of Virginia, and it's important to understand the events leading up to it. Pulitzer Prize–recipient Virginius Dabney, a UVA alumnus, was an author and editor of the *Richmond-Times Dispatch* from 1936 to 1969. Also, his father was a long-serving history professor at UVA. In his 1981 book *Mr. Jefferson's University*, Dabney wrote that coeducation represented "the single most important development in the history of this institution since its early years."[16] And its journey to coeducation, including the multiple times throughout its history where coeducation was considered but not enacted, is also well known. Indeed, in 1996, Supreme Court Associate Justice Ruth Bader Ginsberg wrote in the majority opinion in the case that resulted in the coeducation of Virginia Military Institute, that the state did not have a history of supporting women's higher education, noting "Virginia's protracted fight to exclude women from the University of Virginia prior to 1970."[17]

TWO

UVA'S JOURNEY TO COEDUCATION

The truth will set you free, but first it will piss you off.
—Gloria Steinem

THE UNIVERSITY OF VIRGINIA, founded by Thomas Jefferson in 1819, was, and to some degree still is, steeped in the tradition of "the Virginia Gentleman." The idea of the Virginia gentleman, which goes back several centuries, was something of a plantation-owning, patriarchal ideal—an aristocratic man who embodied honor and gallantry. Jefferson was clear from the start that "The University" was a place where men—white men, that is—would learn in an "Academical Village," carefully designed to place faculty and students in daily contact. This community would enjoy opportunities to learn and live in beauty and architectural splendor, and to this day UVA is considered by many to have the most stunning college campus in the country.

The Grounds is anchored on the north by the Rotunda, a stately building built on a hill. The Rotunda, which housed the original classrooms, is often the first glimpse of the university visitors see. It is majestic on the outside and equally impressive on the inside. Whether you walk through the Rotunda or around it, you come to the Lawn, a vast green space bordered by student rooms and Pavilions, where faculty members work and live. Behind the Pavilions are gardens enclosed by brick serpentine walls and a second group of small rooms called the Range. Usually graduate students or visiting scholars occupy these rooms. The facade of the rear of the Rotunda is as stately as the front, with the same columns and wide portico, and down the Lawn is Cabell Hall. The university, along with Monticello, Jefferson's home, is recognized as one of twenty-four UNESCO World Heritage sites in the United States and draws thousands of visitors yearly, in addition to the students and the university and Charlottesville community, who walk the Grounds and admire the "architectural genius" of the third U.S. president.

The inclusion of women at all-male colleges was not a new idea in the 1960s. Nor was it a new idea at UVA. In fact, it was an idea that had been debated since UVA was established in 1819 and men began attending in 1825. In the book *Going Coed: Women's Experiences in Formerly Men's Colleges and Universities,* Elizabeth Ihle wrote a chapter entitled "Women's Admission to the University of Virginia: Tradition Transformed." In it she wrote that as early as 1880, a faculty committee endorsed the concept of taking more responsibility for "teacher training and the liberal arts education of women either by the adoption of coeducation or the establishment of a coordinate college"—the assumption being, of course, that a woman would be a teacher or nurse, if she worked at all.[1] It is reported that the recommendation was endorsed by the faculty, but they later changed their minds when they seemingly could not find a practical way to implement it. It is important to note that years before women were admitted to the College of Arts and Sciences, women were admitted as transfers into the College of Education and the College of Nursing.

Twelve years later, a woman requested to be examined in mathematics at the university, and the faculty approved her request. Though she scored well on the exam, she was not allowed to attend lectures, and in hindsight the faculty had reservations about the wisdom of their decision to allow her even to take the test. Two years later, they withdrew examination rights, stating "the institution's education was unsuitable to the female sex because it would make women boisterous, bold, and even aggressive, and it would limit their reproductive abilities."[2] The Board of Visitors would support the faculty's decision, stating a refrain that would become common even after our class arrived in 1970: "Coeducation was not in character with the University of Virginia and had not been intended by Thomas Jefferson."

The First Women Admitted

In the early 1900s, the concern about teacher training led to summer programs at the university, and a nursing school was established in 1901. During the next decade the conversation would turn to the establishment of a coordinate school, and it appears that the concept enjoyed wide support. Reports from this time suggest that the coordinate women's school idea implied there would be shared facilities. Despite the endorsement of professional groups and administrators and faculty, students and powerful alumni were opposed. Again, an argument was that it was "contrary to Jefferson's ideals."[3] UVA's first president, Edwin A. Alderman, continued to argue for the establishment of a coordinate college, and it is said that his position of, in essence, supporting women students, although not as progressive as full coeducation, was a step too far for some and "alienated him from some of the students and alumni and cost him trust he never completely regained."[4] The board continued to support the concept until 1917, when war loomed.

Progress was made in 1920 when the university began admitting women to professional schools. Seventeen women comprised the first cadre of female students, many of whom, as reported by Phyllis Leffler in her article "Mr. Jefferson's University: Women in the Village!," "felt they were merely tolerated and not welcomed."[5] Women soon formed a self-government association, which remained until the 1960s, although it appears that its role deteriorated over time. In the late 1920s and 1930s, the idea of a coordinate college, colloquially called a "sister school," would continue to be debated. Then, in 1944, Mary Washington College became the coordinate college of UVA and was renamed Mary Washington College of the University of Virginia. By the 1950s, several hundred women were enrolled at UVA, including transfers in their third and fourth years from Mary Washington College.

By the early 1960s, professors started requesting that their daughters be admitted, which the BOV approved. In 1965, a report from the Virginia Higher Education Study Commission noted in the section on the College of Mary Washington that "there is suspicion in some quarters that the main interest of the University in maintaining College of Mary Washington as a branch with enrollment limited to women students is to prevent pressure for a coeducational program in undergraduate arts and sciences at Charlottesville."[6] There is no indication in the minutes that UVA's Board of Visitors addressed this statement in its January 1966 meeting.[7]

An Eye toward the Ivies

The University of Virginia has been called a "Public Ivy" since Richard Moll coined the term in his 1985 book, *The Public Ivys*. But even in the 1960s, the university was undoubtedly paying close attention to what was happening at elite colleges and universities in the Northeast as many that had all-male enrollment began transitioning to coeducation. As previously noted, UVA paid particular attention when Princeton and Yale began admitting women in 1969. As the 1960s progressed, the nation was rife with controversy, conflict, and change. The Civil Rights Act had been passed in 1964, and the push to end racial discrimination and segregation was a front-page topic in newspapers around the country. What has been referred to as the second wave of feminism was taking hold, and colleges were experiencing unrest. The status quo was being agitated, and the country was at an inflection point. The conversations and actions at Northeast colleges amplified the pressure on UVA administrators to study the coeducation issue.

In 1965, Virginia's governor appointed the Virginia Higher Education Study Commission, which recommended that any new institutions of higher education should be coeducational.[8] They did not address current university programming but were clearly moving in the same direction as other colleges and universities, especially private ones in the Northeast.

UVA Questions Coeducation

In the spring of 1965, the UVA Board of Visitors directed the Committee on the Future of the University (COFU) to study the desirability and feasibility of coeducation at the university. In May 1966, the committee recommended that the university adopt a policy of full coeducation. This was in part motivated by a desire to protect the reputation of the university, which some on the committee felt would be damaged if UVA was forced to coeducate by the courts rather than doing it on their own. Some committee members believed women would seek equal educational opportunities under the Civil Rights Act of 1964 and that legal maneuvering was only a matter of time. The committee also believed this would further the university's plan to increase enrollment, which would enhance UVA's standing as a top university. Ultimately, the committee recommended that UVA admit fifteen thousand students or more by 1980, doubling the 1966 enrollment.

When the COFU report didn't elicit any action, a second subcommittee was formed. In March 1967, the new committee made essentially the same recommendations as the first committee. Again, the committee believed that not acting on coeducation could potentially tarnish the university's national image. According to minutes of the committee, the report stated that the presence of female students "would challenge men to higher achievement in the classrooms and help to create a more normal social climate on the grounds." It further stated, "A university is enriched by the intellectual and emotional interplay between the sexes."[9] The report recommended further study. While these administrative and BOV-sanctioned committees were doing their work, so were student and faculty committees. The student council formed a working group to study and report on coeducation, as did the faculty. Once the BOV passed the resolutions, articles in the *Cavalier Daily* about the prospect of coeducation increased, and in some camps, battle lines were drawn.

According to an April 11, 1967, article from the *Cavalier Daily*, in a small, twenty-six-student survey, only two students were reported to support coeducation. Minutes from a University-sanctioned meeting on April 11, 1968, state that in informal talks with students "independents favored admission [of women] while Fraternity men, presumably because they dominated the present set-up, were opposed."[10]

Women matriculating at UVA in the mid- to late 1960s were almost all in nursing, education, and graduate schools. In an article in the September 29, 1967, issue of the *Cavalier Daily* titled "Whitney Sees Gain for Men, Women in Co-Education," Mary Whitney (UVA dean of women from 1967 to 1970) stated, "It is important that men and women be able to benefit from each other during the educational experience. That's only natural." She stated further that she is "very biased about co-education," having never experienced any other kind of college environment. The article continues, however, with mixed reactions from women students. While some indicated full support for coeducation, others had their doubts. "It would ruin the intellectual atmosphere and lower the standing," one woman suggested. "It wouldn't look right," another woman said.

In April 1967, President Edgar Shannon took the COFU reports to the Board of Visitors. David Salem, Shannon's son-in-law, wrote a 1998 monograph about Shannon's tenure as UVA's president. In it, he wrote that Shannon's private belief "that admitting women was essential to become 'a great university'" was not shared by all members; however, it was evident to most members that it "seemed only a matter of time before the University would come under attack for keeping its doors closed to women undergraduates. If the University dawdled long enough, it would, in the private opinion of Rector Frank Rogers (a prominent lawyer) be forced to admit women whether it wanted to or not." Shannon, believing in a grassroots process, nonetheless felt that "it was critical that the University admit women voluntarily, before it was ordered to do so by the courts."[11]

On April 8, 1967, the Board of Visitors adopted the following resolution:

RESOLVED by the Rector and Visitors of the University of Virginia that the President be and he is hereby empowered to conduct a study to determine whether there is a need for the admission of women to the College of Arts and Sciences in Charlottesville:

RESOLVED FURTHER that if the study should establish the existence of need for such admission, the President be and have is hereby empowered to conduct a study of the feasibility and means of such admission; and

RESOLVED FURTHER that the findings of the study or studies be presented to the Board of Visitors for its consideration.[12]

In essence, is there a need to admit women to UVA? If so, what is the feasibility of admitting women, and what are the best means by which to do that? And lastly, whatever the committee discovers should be presented to the BOV for their consideration.

Under the direction of the BOV, President Shannon appointed a ten-member committee limited to the study of just the first question: *Is there a need to admit women to UVA?* He appointed Lewis H. Hammond, chairman of the Department of Philosophy, to chair this committee, which was tasked with studying the possible admission of women to the College of Arts and Sciences at the University of Virginia at Charlottesville.[13] The nine other members were carefully selected to include seven UVA faculty members, four of whom were UVA graduates, plus two who were from the faculty of the College of Mary Washington, which at that point was affiliated with and under the direction of UVA's Board of Visitors. There was little question on the part of the BOV and others that Mary Washington would be greatly impacted if UVA admitted women to undergraduate programs in the College of Arts and Sciences. In the May 26, 1967, letter appointing Professor Hammond to the committee chairmanship, President Shannon states, "This study is of the highest importance to the University. I am indeed grateful to you and to your associates for undertaking it."[14] Hammond and the committee began their work. On June 22, 1967, in a response to questions posed by the chair about the legality of a male-only undergraduate program, C. Venable Minor, special counsel for the rector and visitors of the University of Virginia wrote:

> I am of the opinion that the question of admission of women to the College of Arts and Sciences of the University of Virginia is one of policy within the discretion of the Board of Visitors and that there is no statute or case law requiring such admission. I am further of the opinion that there are no provisions of the Civil Rights Act of 1964 which prohibit discrimination as to sex with respect to such admission. While it is, of course, possible that a suit might be brought against the University to require admission of women I am doubtful that any such suit would be successful, in that there

are other state-supported institutions of learning in the state of Virginia such as William and Mary, Virginia Polytechnic Institute, Longwood College and Mary Washington College, [which is part] of the University itself, which are open to them.[15]

The Woody Committee

Professor Hammond suffered a heart attack that summer, and although he survived, he vacated the committee; on September 30, 1967, T. Braxton Woody, assistant dean of students, was tapped to chair the committee (which became known colloquially as "The Woody Committee"). Woody was an alumnus of UVA with admittedly deep roots. He was perceived as a traditionalist and was conservative in nature. According to minutes of committee meetings, their work included surveying faculty, alumni, and some student groups and organizations. Each member of the committee wrote a position paper, and correspondence indicates that opinions were actively sought by engaging with student and university organizations.[16]

But then, according to my research, at the April 11, 1968, committee meeting, Woody used an offensive slur when referring to Jewish people.[17] In response, Albert R. Klein and James H. Croushore, the two committee members representing the College of Mary Washington, resigned. Croushore was not in attendance at the meeting but apparently resigned in solidarity with his colleague. Despite Woody's apology and President Shannon's plea for the two members to rejoin the committee, including a trip to Fredericksburg to meet personally with Croushore, who over the summer had been promoted to dean, Klein and Croushore refused to rescind their resignations. On April 15, 1968, Woody sent the following letter to Albert Klein:

Dear Mr. Klein:

It is my sincere hope that you will accept my apology for the heedless remarks I made at the last meeting of our committee. Once again let me assure you that I never use the word "Kike" to refer to the Jewish race, for which I have the greatest esteem, but only for certain members of that race who by their actions make themselves objectionable. Please consider also that I spoke in most favorable terms of the fine class of Jewish boys we have had the good fortune to attract to the University of Virginia in recent years. I value the friendship of many of them whom I have come to know quite well.

I await earnestly your acceptance of my sincere apology and your reconsideration of your resignation from our committee.

Sincerely yours,
T. Braxton Woody

On April 22, 1968, President Shannon sent letters to both men.

Dear Professor Klein:

I regret very much that any statements by the Chairman of the special Committee to consider admission of women to the College of Arts and Sciences at Charlottesville made you feel that you ought to offer your resignation from the Committee. The Chairman has expressed his distress over any remarks that could be interpreted as derogatory. Since he has expressed his apologies to you over the telephone and in writing, I hope very much that you will feel it possible to reconsider your decision and that you will be willing to continue to serve on the Committee.

Both the Chairman and I value greatly the contribution that you and Mr. Croushore are making to the Committee. I feel that it would be most unfortunate for all of us if your continuity of service and background of experience were lost to the Committee.

Sincerely yours,
Edgar F. Shannon, Jr.
President

Dear Mr. Croushore:

As I said in my brief conversation with you at Mary Washington, I regret exceedingly that any discussion in the special Committee on the Admission of Women to the College of Arts and Sciences at Charlottesville could have led you to feel that you could make no further contribution to the work of the Committee. The Chairman of the Committee has expressed his regrets and apologies to Mr. Klein, both by telephone and in writing, and has written to you as well. As I have told Mr. Klein, I am extremely sorry that any implications in the discussion could have arisen that created pain or embarrassment to him or to you. I am convinced that this was the farthest from the intention of the Chairman.

Both the Committee and I value greatly the contribution that you and Mr. Klein have been making to the Committee. It is much to be desired for the good of both Mary Washington and the University that you and he continue on the Committee.

I hope very much that you will reconsider your decision and will be willing to resume your service.

Sincerely yours,
Edgar F. Shannon, Jr.
President

On April 26, 1968, James Croushore responded:

Dear President Shannon:

Many, many times during the last two days, for the sake of professional, institutional, and personal ties I have wanted to say that I would continue serving on the special committee on the Admission of Women to the College of Arts and Sciences; but I feel that any committee report to you will be so fraught with significance and so important to our two institutions that I dare not risk causing or being the cause of any departure from dispassionate and objective inquiry.

I appreciate deeply your serious concern, and I want you to know that I reply as I do because I believe that men of good-will have control of their personal value system, but that they do not necessarily have as complete control as they would wish over the way that value system colors judgments. Because I recognize this limitation in myself, I feel sincerely that I must re-affirm my previous decision.

Sincerely,
James H. Croushore
Associate Dean

Penciled onto Croushore's original letter to President Shannon, archived with other documents from this time, is the following note: "These two-bit freaks ought to be teaching in a kindergarten. F.L.B." This comment was apparently written by Shannon's assistant, Francis L. Berkley Jr., who also penciled in filing instructions on this letter and much of the correspondence I reviewed.

On April 27 Klein responded:

Dear President Shannon:

Thank you for your letter asking me to rejoin the special Committee to consider admission of women to the College of Arts and Sciences at Charlottesville. I have already replied to the Chairman that I was unable to return. My position with the committee altered the moment I was confronted with what I felt were discriminatory remarks. My ideas and expressions would now be emotionally and intellectually inconsistent with whatever service I might give to the committee.

Again, I thank you for your letter indicating your continued wish to have me serve on the committee, but I feel I must not return.

Sincerely yours,
Albert R. Klein
Professor of Dramatic Arts and Speech

Tragically, Albert Klein died in an automobile accident on October 6, 1970. On October 22, 1971, the College of Mary Washington renamed and dedicated the main theater on campus in his memory and for his "rich contribution to the college."[18] It remains named for him to this day. James Croushore died in 1995, and the archivist at Mary Washington in 2022 reported they have no archival papers from either man that include their time on the committee.

According to the minutes of the May 16, 1968, committee meeting, Woody read the letters of resignation of the two Mary Washington members, and he announced the tragic death of another committee member. The final committee report referenced a seven-member committee, not the ten members appointed by President Shannon.

Looking back, it didn't bode well that the chair of the committee tasked with potentially ushering in a new era of progress was himself exhibiting bigotry. Or that President Shannon's assistant penciled in the derogatory comment about the Mary Washington faculty members on Croushore's original letter to Shannon.

Students, Faculty, and Alumni Weigh In

The committee continued to gather the opinion of students, faculty, and alumni.[19] The 1968 April–May issue of the *University of Virginia Topics* contained a green box with the following text: "WOMEN? A special committee appointed by President Shannon is eager to receive the views of alumni on the admission of women to the College of Arts and Sciences." This communication, sent as part of a regular newsletter to forty thousand alumni, yielded ninety-eight responses, overwhelmingly against admitting women.

Examples of some of the responses received from alumni are included below.[20] The comments may seem incredibly archaic in light of today's cultural norms, and it's possible some were an attempt at humor. Nonetheless, some alumni not only shared their displeasure with the idea of coeducation but also threatened withdrawal of future financial support.

> Some of my best friends are women. I love women. My mother is a woman. So is my secretary . . . Could a woman play lacrosse or right guard on the football team? Think of the *Cavalier Daily* city room with a female reporter at the typewriter, cigarette dangling from her lips. Could professors conscientiously commence lectures with "Gentlemen"? Visualize a face-gooed coed in curlers and robe scuttling from West Range to the head. Women at Openings, Midwinters and Easters, to be sure. But in the College? Yecck!

> I feel confident that if the students themselves were polled, the male students would prefer their present autonomy while the females, bless their little hearts, would be overwhelmingly in favor of the increased opportunity to secure a husband at an earlier age.

> Pox on women!

> These are the qualities which must not be lost: The lingering quality of a gentleman's club with its discussion of fraternity, philosophy, politick, and folly-of-the-flesh. Modernization of the university into still another large,

co-educational institution threatens this basic goodness. So, I propose that the quality of women accepted, and their program of orientation, be of a high enough caliber to instill in them a love of tradition and an understanding of the University. Speaking practically, the Honor Code must be made clear, embibed [sic], and strictly enforced among the women. They seem more inclined toward lying, cheating and stealing than men. It must be made clear that they cannot steal from one another in the dorms or classroom. It must be made clear that they cannot cheat on exams or attempt to beguile professors or gentlemen into dishonesty.

My reasons, I confess, are selfish. In my experience (which has been confirmed by others with whom I have discussed this matter) literature majors at co-educational institutions are almost invariably dominated by the women. Here at Rice, for example, where I am visiting this year, the proportion of men to women in the college as a whole is two to one: yet with regard to the English major, this ratio is exactly reversed—or rather it is closer to the ratio of three to one, the women being in the majority. This situation has a number of unhappy effects; for one thing, the study of literature comes to be regarded as some sort of exclusively feminine pursuit, the ablest young men feeling obliged to flee to history or philosophy if they want to remain in the Humanities at all: furthermore, though I find that women are generally more conscientious and reliable than men, they are rarely as brilliant or as dazzling in creative ways as the best young men I have taught.

The faculty responses, while not large in number, were overwhelmingly supportive of coeducation. This would become important after women were admitted and male faculty members created much of the tension and discomfort women reported encountering during their initial months.

> I do hope women will be admitted on a truly coeducational basis. Separation of the classes under some sort of coordinate education would create second-class students, faculty and scholarship.

> It seems to me that this university might adopt a policy similar to that of Stanford University, where I have taught on two occasions. At least a number of years ago Stanford admitted 500 undergraduate women. They are of course an outstanding group just as such a selected number would be at this

university. This group would serve to elevate the general level of academic achievement and would at the same time help to normalize the social life on the grounds. For these two reasons, therefore, I believe that the university would benefit from a limited coeducational policy.

I feel strongly that there *is* a need for admission of women to the College of Arts and Sciences at Charlottesville. There are two compelling reasons for such admission it seems to me. First, it is a point of obvious discrimination to prevent women from availing themselves of the best educational facilities in the Commonwealth. No other public institution provides such facilities, certainly not the "separate but equal" arrangement implied in the operation of Mary Washington College. In this respect, I presume we are operating outside the law in these matters. Quite aside from the legal question is that we have responsibilities to educate young Virginians and young Americans whatever their sex. Secondly, it seems to me that a natural academic climate requires the presence of women. It is unrealistic, if not archaic, to assume that a male student body is the ideal academic situation in which to pursue scholarship and intellectual excellence. We have demonstrated this quite amply in our professional schools and the Graduate School, and it is not necessary therefore to see what Harvard, or Yale, etc. are doing in these matters. The best of my graduate students in this university have been women.

I believe male or female educational institutions are unnatural, undesirable, and anachronistic. In addition, the inclusion of females in our list of applicants would introduce more competition and raise our standards immediately. To me, it is highly desirable to *encourage* women to attend UVA.

Admit them! Let's catch up to the 20th century.

A professor of psychology at UVA's School of Medicine supported coeducation, but the reasons he gave are hard to read. His response states in part:

As a Psychologist and working with mental health problems in college students and the general community, I find that the most outstanding problems with not having women here at the University is that we have many sexual identification problems occurring in the University men. These problems generally blossom up in the form of homosexual patterns for these boys. The other major way that these problems manifest themselves is the relationship that these boys establish with girls from "down the road" or with townees.

He continues, "In short, I believe that a steady diet of women would avert some of the psychological and social problems created by a limited diet of them."

The alumni would later complain that their opinions were not solicited, some apparently not reading the newsletter and others indicating that this was not a sufficient nor effective means of gathering this information. Woody would meet with alumni prior to the BOV meeting where the Woody Report would be presented, seemingly to appease them and give them further voice to the divisive and emotional issue of coeducation. To be clear, although the alumni responses are difficult to read and even more difficult to understand, their sentiments were not isolated. Lynn Peril, in her book *College Girls: Bluestockings, Sex Kittens, and Coeds, Then and Now*, reports that there was an "assumption that college girls trolled for men rather than study."[21]

Annette Gibbs, who would be appointed in the spring of 1970 as associate dean of student affairs said:

> I know the early criticisms were that this place was only going to attract two types of women students. One, those who were quote "raging feminists," whatever that meant at the time. And secondly, those who were, quote, "just looking for husbands," unquote. And, to tell the truth, that was never an overt or a silent observation on my part. Women who came here in those early years were very similar to the men who came here. They were interested in the University's academic program, and they were interested in the University's quality of life experience as an undergraduate.[22]

In a rather strange twist, the committee believed that it would not be possible to survey the entire student body, so student opinion was derived from a few organizations who were asked to weigh in. These included the Honor Committee, whose members took a strong position against coeducation, and the Raven Society, the oldest honorary group at the university. There was a sharp divide between the undergraduate and graduate student responses, with the older students considerably more in favor of coeducation.[23] Some believe that the inclusion of women students in the professional and graduate schools for more than forty-five years facilitated male graduate students' familiarity and comfort with women classmates. And as was noted previously, from the first rumblings of coeducation and subsequent committee work, students made their opinions known. Despite the limited numbers of students officially polled by the committee studying the admission of women, their responses would indicate that students supported coeducation.

Cochairs of the Coeducation Committee of the Martin Luther King, Jr. Chapter of the Virginia Council on Human Relations sent a letter to President Shannon expressing concern that no students were on the Woody Committee and that the committee did not "solicit the opinion of a representative sample of students." They further stated, "While student leaders were consulted, these were mainly fraternity men. . . . VCHR feels that full coeducation at the University is necessary not only because women are legally entitled to an equal education in Virginia, but also because the increased social opportunities that would follow coeducation would make the University more attractive to the most qualified students in the nation, both black and white."[24]

The committee issued its report in December 1968. The report, often referred to as the "Woody Report," only dealt with the first part of the question posed about coeducation—Is there a "need to coeducate?"[25] The report was overwhelmingly favorable toward coeducation, with a vote of 6 to 1 of the then seven-member committee. The dissenting vote, Mr. Bischoff, wrote a minority report that is appended in the full report along with a treatise from the Honor Committee taking a strong stand against coeducation.[26] The Honor Committee's opposition was based, in part, on a study conducted at Cornell University suggesting that honor codes at coeducated schools are only half as effective as ones at all-male schools. It should be noted that then, and now, the veracity of the Cornell paper has been questioned.

The overwhelmingly positive report examined the moral implications of denying admission to women. The report stated, in part, "Perhaps we are not yet legally obligated to admit women, but is it morally right, is it defensible in the name of justice, to discriminate against them on grounds of sex?" The committee did not take a position on what had been termed in the *Cavalier Daily* and elsewhere as "the inferiority of Mary Washington College."[27] The soon-to-be-filed lawsuit, however, asserted that an education at Mary Washington was not on par with an education at UVA.[28] This statement, both in print in the student newspaper and in the lawsuit, would cost UVA goodwill for years to come and highlighted, to some, UVA's reputation for elitism and arrogance.

Despite the positive report and the publicly stated belief that coeducation was the morally right path forward, the underlying sentiments of individual members, including Chairman Woody, appear to be more complicated. In a January 6, 1969, letter to Thomas B. Gay, an alumnus who took a highly vocal stand against coeducation, Braxton Woody writes, in part, "The members of our committee are very appreciative of the interest you have shown in our study of the admission of women to the College. If the recommendations of our report run counter to your convictions, and I greatly fear they do, it is not as much that we oppose your views as that we believe the many changes of the past fifty years have made coeducation inevitable, if not entirely desirable."[29]

Tami Lynn Curtis, in a master's thesis about UVA's coeducation process, examined committee minutes and other documents and concluded, "The Woody committee supported admission of women for three main reasons: 1) as a prescription to meet the needs of young men, 2) as necessary to the development of a modern, prestigious university, and 3) as a necessary means of avoiding legal compulsion. The committee did not recommend admission because a consensus existed that accepted the intellectual capabilities of women as equal to those of men."[30] She also notes that around this time, Jo Anne Kirstein, who would later file suit with three other women and the United States National Student Association, met with Woody and told him that she would be attending the university the following year, either through the committee's actions or a lawsuit.

At the December meeting of the BOV, President Shannon was tasked with forming a committee to explore the second item on the BOV's 1967 resolution, the feasibility and means of coeducation. Shannon appointed Frank Hereford, then the provost, to chair this committee.[31] Under his leadership, the committee submitted their report in January, and the report was approved by the BOV on February 15, 1969.

Dean of Women

During this time in UVA's history, the administrative team included a dean of women, a position that was only held by four women. The position would be eliminated, effective July 1970, in a move many saw as retribution, as the last woman to hold the position, Mary Whitney, was actively engaged in the support of coeducation and also testified in the lawsuit.[32] Whitney was dean of women from July 1, 1967, until June 30, 1970, replacing Roberta Gwathmey, who was an alumna of UVA and tapped for the position temporarily when she was pursuing a doctorate in romance languages.

Roberta Hollingsworth Gwathmey served as dean of women for thirty-three years, from 1934 to 1967, at one point with fewer than eighty female students at the University.[33] The archived papers of Gwathmey contain correspondence about the Women's Student Association, formed in 1920 to self-govern women and social functions. It appears from Gwathmey's correspondence that in her role, she intervened when there was conflict with a woman and also provided "gentle" advocacy for women students. One example is an issue of housing for a Black female teacher, who, in 1961, was selected to participate in a National Science Foundation Academic Year Institute (AYI) in the education school. The teacher requested housing at the dorm Mary Munford, along with the other female participants. In a memo sent to President Shannon by Gwathmey's assistant, she indicates that this was an unacceptable request and suggests that Gwathmey talk with the woman and help find her placement in a private home, as she had done before in similar situations.[34]

The memo reads, in part, "This woman, [last name redacted] was offered participation in the A.Y.I. on the assumption that since she has a ten-year-old girl, she would be taking an apartment and the question of University housing would not arise. She has apparently decided to leave her little girl behind and has applied for living accommodations in the dormitory." The memo then cites cases of two other Black applicants in which a personal interview "removed the problem." The implication was that they found other housing. The response to the memo to President Shannon was from B. F. D. Runk, who indicated that he had consulted with the special counsel for the university, and "denials of such applications cannot be made on the basis of race." The applicant was to be offered accommodations at Mary Munford Hall.

Correspondence from 1962 between Gwathmey and Ralph Cherry, dean of the School of Education, indicated that the education school was planning to discontinue admitting first- and second-year students, acknowledging that the move would affect a "small number of young women who would be ineligible for admission to the University if this step is taken." Cherry continues, "I can assure you that it is not our desire nor intention to decrease the number of women students in the University. On the other hand, we believe that the University should be willing to accept qualified women students in the College of Arts and Sciences."[35]

Gwathmey responds, in part, "You probably know that I have always felt extremely sympathetic over the position in which the School of Education as a professional school has been placed by the fact that it has been the only door open to undergraduate women students, while at the same time being grateful for the help this afforded girls who had good reason to be here, either because of their families, their husbands, or employment."

In 1967, Mary Whitney was hired to replace the retiring Gwathmey. Little is written about Whitney, nor do the archival files contain much that helps us understand her tenure at UVA. She did, however, write a comprehensive manuscript, "Women and the University," which chronicles the history of women from the founding of the university until the report's completion in 1969.[36] Whitney relates that the project took her six months to research and that it presents "the history of the coeducation question at the University of Virginia." Whitney references this manuscript in a 1969 end-of-year report she filed with D. Alan Williams, dean of student affairs, and it still can be found on the shelves in the reading room of UVA's Small Special Collections Library. Her last report hints at the tension she faced in her role, only made worse when she openly advocated for coeducation.

Whitney's report started with the current enrollment numbers in

1969: 1,168 total women in attendance; 333 undergraduate and 835 graduate, with 38 percent living on Grounds.[37] Then she cuts right to the chase:

> The problems handled for the women students attending the University during the 1969 Spring semester were similar to those problems handled during previous semesters, except for one—security. Increasingly the need to perform additional security measures for the women students became more apparent during the 1969 spring semester. During the Spring, I wrote numerous letters to the women outlining hints and tips they should follow for their own security; I responded to a number of night calls involving women who had been attacked, molested, and/or raped; and I continued to plead and beg for more lights in dark areas on the Grounds and in the City of Charlottesville. I might add here that I am still taking every opportunity to persuade "the powers that be" to spend more money on more and better lights on the Grounds.

Her report continues:

> The 1969 spring semester also marked a turning point in trying to persuade others to allow women equal access to the College of Arts and Sciences. In January, I served on a Coeducational Sub-Committee of the Committee on the Future of the University. The Sub-Committee's report and the full committee's endorsement was submitted to the Board of Visitors on February 1, 1969, with one important recommendation, that Charlottesville and Albemarle women be allowed admission to the College in September, 1969. Regretably, [sic] the Board did not act on this recommendation. I felt strongly and still do that if the Board of Visitors had agreed to and passed this particular recommendation, it would not have been subsequently sued in a Federal Court.

Whitney's report discusses her decision to resign her position:

> One of the most difficult things during the 1969 spring semester was the emotions held by many at the University about coeducation. Everywhere I went and every formal meeting in which I participated meant some form of discussion about coeducation. I was particularly distressed when this topic and the emotions surrounding it entered my social life. After the third

dinner party I attended, in which I was discourteously accused of being responsible for the "evil" of coeducation, I decided to submit my resignation, doing so on May 16, 1969. During the ensuing months I have not regretted my resignation although many have told me that they thought I was foolish for taking such an action. I do not feel that I was, nor do I feel that my leaving or staying will make much difference in the admission to and position of the woman student at U.Va. I think the University of Virginia will continue to drag its feet, so to speak, when it comes to the women students. Despite its being forced to do something by a Federal Court, I think the University will still practice a form of mass resistance toward women for a long time to come.

Whitney's report continues with more actions and concerns around safety and lighting and states that in the fall she began working to help prepare for additional women students. Her report continues:

My office assistant inspected the women's restrooms on the Grounds, and then I wrote various individuals requesting that a number of improvements be made in these restrooms. I particularly requested that sanitary napkin machines be installed in every woman's restroom on the Grounds. At this writing, I have received no response from this particular memorandum, except one from the Dean of Students endorsing my request. Certainly, the request for sanitary napkin machines is not outrageous, but the non-response or what I call avoidance behavior is one more piece of evidence for the University's resistance against women.

Whitney's report indicates lack of activities for women, lack of adequate recreational facilities, and concern about responses she received when surveying women who matriculated in September 1968. Although she had not completed the analysis of all the responses, she indicated that "almost fifty percent of the women surveyed have not enjoyed their tenure at the University of Virginia, academically, although they have socially. One reason given by the students for their academic disappointment was the discrimination demonstrated and practiced toward them in classes taught by male professors." Whitney mentions that she "was also subpoenaed to testify in the ACLU suit against the University." Her report ends with no recommendations, since, she says, "I will leave the University of Virginia on June 30, 1970."

In his annual report to Shannon, D. Alan Williams, the dean of student affairs, references Whitney's report, writing, "The report of Dean Mary Whitney is self-explanatory. It reflects the personality of the Dean and her apprehension about coeducation." This statement does not include the reason for Whitney's apprehension, if indeed that is a fair description. From all archival documentation examined, it appears Whitney, like many, doubted that the current administration was highly motivated to coeducate. She lacked faith in the commitment of UVA's administrators and student organizations to welcoming women and ensuring their transition into university life.

Philip J. Hirschkop, a civil rights attorney from Alexandria, Virginia, and one of the lawyers for the plaintiffs in the pivotal ACLU lawsuit (more on that to come), would later speak to the role Whitney played in the lawsuit. He is quoted as saying that Mary Whitney is the "hidden hero of the whole case." She is credited with assisting the legal team behind the scenes, as well as recruiting three of the plaintiffs.[38] While it is understood that Whitney left UVA after she resigned her position, it is clear that she played a key role in bringing about coeducation through the lawsuit.

Whitney died in 2013 and her obituary reads, in part, "She was Dean of Women at the University of Virginia 1967–70. Her monograph on the struggle for women to gain admission as regular students was instrumental in overturning the university's anti-coeducational policy. But it also led to her resignation."[39]

In addition to Mary Whitney's efforts, student support for coeducation was gaining momentum in the late 1960s. On February 16, 1969, a coalition of organizations convened at the Rotunda over several days to protest the war and bring attention to issues that they felt required action from UVA's administration. The Student Coalition, as it was named, presented eleven "demands" to President Shannon, primarily civil rights issues. Coeducation was one of the demands, although it was not included on the plaque erected in 2020 on Grounds to commemorate this event.[40]

UVA's "May Days," protests in response to the war in Vietnam, usurped the planning for the September 1970 arrival of women. (*Corks and Curls* photo archive)

A little more than a year later, similar demands, including coeducation, would be presented again to Shannon in what would later be called "The May Day Strike."

Rumblings of a Lawsuit

Before the lawsuit was filed, there were clear indications that leaders at UVA knew one was a possibility. It appears that both Whitney and Ern had information that forecasted the potential of a lawsuit. On a Saturday morning in March 1969, Ern met with prospective student Virginia Scott, a resident of Charlottesville, who would become a plaintiff in the lawsuit. She wished to enroll in the 1969 first-year class, and on the interview form Ern completed after meeting with her, he noted, "Secretary to John Lowe—wants to bring suit thru ACLU."[41] And in Whitney's 1969 end-of-year report, referenced above, she noted that if local women had been allowed to enroll, there would have likely been no lawsuit.

Although the general counsel for the university had determined that UVA's admission policy was not against the law, and if challenged, the challenge would not likely be upheld, Shannon, who was not a lawyer, had his doubts. Behind the scenes, Shannon was urging that coeducation move forward posthaste.[42] Some believed that he wasn't vocal enough about his backing of coeducation, but others say he was in fact incredibly strategic in his role in the process. For example, by selecting T. Braxton Woody to chair the committee after the first chair resigned, he ensured that, in the words of Richard Gard, "a dyed-in-the-herringbone-tweed-traditionalist" and an alumnus would lead the work.[43] Shannon trusted Woody to present what the committee members determined to be the best action regarding the issue of coeducation at UVA. That would give credibility to what Shannon believed was the inevitable conclusion, that is, that coeducation was desirable and, yes, necessary, to further the progress of the university. In my 2021 interview with Ern, he said there was little doubt that Shannon favored coeducation. "He was the father of five daughters," Ern chuckled.

Although Shannon may have hoped that the university would move toward coeducation, many alumni were opposed. Years later, B. F. D. Runk, a colleague and friend of Woody's, as well as a fellow alumnus, related, as part of an oral history project, his dismay at the committee's report and Woody's endorsement of coeducation. "I'm just as happy that I wasn't asked to serve on that committee because I just don't like coeducation at the University of Virginia. To me, it isn't part of the University, on the undergraduate level. Ever since I was a student here, we had graduate women in graduate arts and sciences, for example, education and the like. I think that the University of Virginia has lost some of its uniqueness by going coeducation. Being one of the old school, I don't like this." When asked by the oral history interviewer, "Was there a dichotomy in the administration on it?" Runk responded:

> I thought that Braxton Woody was on my side; I was astounded when his report came out that he, as Chairman of the committee, was in favor of letting the bars down and admitting women to the undergraduate schools of the University. Yes, there was a dichotomy. I'm afraid, however that the

President and Mrs. Shannon with their five daughters.
(*The First Year Directory of the Class of 1974*)

"old guard" had gotten so thin in numbers that the new people took over. The younger members of the faculty were all for coeducation and all of those that had not been University of Virginia students.[44]

There are a number of accounts of Runk making his sentiments about coeducation known, often speaking of women in a derogatory manner.

Even though from all accounts President Shannon was in support of coeducation at UVA and had charged committees with studying the issue, he was not able to head off the lawsuit. His son-in-law David wrote years later that Shannon regretted not moving more quickly on coeducation, thus avoiding litigation. His eldest daughter, Eleanor Shannon, spoke with me after attending the April 5, 2024, dedication of the university library, which has been renovated and renamed the Shannon Library. During the dedication ceremony President Shannon's leadership in integrating and coeducating the university was noted. Eleanor reflected on those years:

Some say the coeducation journey for him was about his five daughters. But it was much more than that. My mother was a smart, academic woman and she and my father met after she had been the Dean of Women at what is now Rhodes College in Memphis and was working on her doctorate at Columbia University. His mother was also an academic, assisting his father, an English professor at Washington and Lee [University], with his research and writing projects. But the bigger reason my father felt so strongly about coeducation was that he truly believed you could not have a great university without the diversity of races, ethnicities, religions, and genders.

Lawsuit Changes Everything

In May 1969, the lawsuit, *Mrs. Jo Anne Kirstein, et al., and the United States National Student Association v. The Rector and Visitors of the University of Virginia, et al.*, was filed in the U.S. District Court for the Eastern District of Virginia in Richmond.[45] Hirschkop and Lowe, working on behalf of the American Civil Liberties Union (ACLU), represented four young females and the U.S. National Student Association. As noted previously, Mary Whitney helped identify the plaintiffs in the case and provided support to the legal team. The lawsuit was a class action suit, meaning it would benefit a larger group or "class," and in this case, it was filed on behalf of all women—"other women in the State of Virginia who desire an education at the College of Arts and Sciences of the University of Virginia and who have been explicitly denied admission because of sex or have been discouraged to apply because of their knowledge of the College's admissions policy." It then cited other state institutions of higher education that also "exclude applicants on the basis of sex."

In a particularly compelling and damning statement, the lawsuit stated, "The foregoing schools are state institutions operating under color of state law. Their practices, customs and policies in maintaining sexual segregation are without rational basis or foundation in law. They are purely vestiges of archaic and constitutionally outmoded customs and doctrines of male superiority not consonant with modern western civilization. Indeed, they violate all modern precepts of education an overwhelming trend in even private sectors of education to co-educational institutions."

AUG 11 1969

IN THE

UNITED STATES DISTRICT COURT

FOR THE

EASTERN DISTRICT OF VIRGINIA

Richmond Division

MRS. JO ANNE KIRSTEIN,   )
MISS VIRGINIA ANNE SCOTT,   )
MISS NANCY L. ANDERSON,   )
MRS. NANCY JAFFE, and   )
UNITED STATES NATIONAL STUDENT   )
    ASSOCIATION,   )
)
            Plaintiffs,   )
)
v.   )   CIVIL ACTION NO.
)   220-69-R
THE RECTOR AND VISITORS OF THE   )
    UNIVERSITY OF VIRGINIA, etc.,)
THE HONORABLE MILLS E. GODWIN,   )
DR. WOODROW W. WILKERSON,   )
EDGAR F. SHANNON, JR.,   )
ERNEST H. ERN, and   )
STATE COUNCIL OF HIGHER EDUCATION)
    FOR VIRGINIA,   )
)
            Defendants.   )

PLAINTIFFS' BRIEF ON THE MERITS

                          PHILIP J. HIRSCHKOP, Esquire
                             American Civil Liberties Union
                               of Virginia
                             110 North Royal Street
                             P. O. Box 234
                             Alexandria, Virginia 22313
                             703-836-5550

                          JOHN C. LOWE, Esquire
                             American Civil Liberties Union
                               of Virginia
                             414 Park Street
                             Charlottesville, Virginia 22901
                             703-296-8199

OF COUNSEL:

MICHAEL NUSSBAUM, Esquire
    Surrey, Karasik, Gould and Greene
    1156 Fifteenth Street, N. W.
    Washington, D. C. 20005

First page of the history-making lawsuit that led to the admission of women to the University of Virginia.

The lawsuit summarized the argument, in part:

Plaintiffs contend that:

1. The Equal Protection Clause of the Fourteenth Amendment is not solely for the protection of Negroes but has been expanded to protect all classes of citizens from arbitrary and invidious discrimination.

2. Women, in light of their special status in society, constitute a class deserving of equal protection of the laws.

. . . Finally, plaintiffs contend that, as a result of the inferiority of the all-female institutions, they have been denied their constitutionally protected right to learn, inherent in the fundamental and constitutional rights of academic freedom, free speech and freedom of association. Also, inasmuch as they are being denied the opportunity to exchange new and different ideas, plaintiffs allege that their precious First Amendment freedoms of speech and association are being unnecessarily abridged.

The university believed the lawsuit was moot since the BOV had already voted to coeducate.[46] Provost Frank L. Hereford Jr. chaired the committee on the Feasibility and Means of the Admission of Women to the College/Committee on the Future of the University and, taking into consideration a number of the issues about which alumni especially were concerned, presented the plan to President Shannon. It stated, "The ultimate goal should be a ratio of men to women which preserves the traditions of the University and which provides the optimum educational experience for the students within this framework."[47] It went on to say that, initially, the number of women admitted should be "carefully phased" because "the number of qualified male applicants admitted should not be curtailed as a result of the admission of women," as well as to ensure that the university's faculty and facilities were not overburdened. This plan was continually being refined during the spring of 1969 and included a strict quota system that would cap female enrollment at 35 percent in undergraduate programs.

In the meantime, at a preliminary hearing in September 1969, Judge Robert R. Merhige Jr., the judge assigned to the case, issued a temporary injunction sought by the ACLU that would allow the four plaintiffs to apply for admission and, if accepted, attend classes that September.[48] It is reported that of the four, two were offered admission, and only Virginia Scott enrolled.

While it has been reported that Scott (Arts and Sciences, '73; Grad. Arts and Sciences, '80; M.Ed., '89) was the first female first-year student at UVA, that is not the case. In 1968, four female undergraduate students were enrolled in the College of Arts and Sciences, and at least one was a first-year student. Regardless, Virginia Scott and her fellow plaintiffs unequivocally opened the doors for women to matriculate in the College of Arts and Sciences.

The student council was approached by the plaintiffs' attorneys and asked to file an amicus brief supporting the lawsuit. An amicus brief is potentially helpful information provided by an individual, group, or organization that is not directly involved in a legal case. In a close vote, the student council decided against such a move, fearing alienation from the administration. Kevin Mannix (Arts and Sciences, '71; Law, '74), a third-year student and member of the student council, had been appointed as the only undergraduate on the second coeducation committee, known as the Hereford Committee, evaluating the feasibility and means of coeducation at the college. The committee wrote a report that called for a quota system for ten years, with consideration, but no guarantee, as to equal admission after that time. Mannix wrote a one-person minority report that called for the immediate equal admission of women, which the student council endorsed and became an official report from that body.

The court met three weeks later, and in the morning prior to the afternoon hearing, the judges attempted to get the parties to settle. They did not succeed. The afternoon session was reportedly a disaster for the university, with Provost Frank Hereford defending the university's plan, which was complex and allegedly impenetrable. At that time, the court was also presented with Mannix's Minority Report appended to the University's report.[49] The university had not submitted the Minority Report, but Mannix gave it to John Lowe (lawyer and former boss of plaintiff Virginia A. Scott), who brought it to court, asking Hereford if he recognized it. He did. The rest is history.

UVA's Plan to Coeducate

On October 1, 1969, the U.S. District Court for the Eastern District of Virginia instructed UVA to submit a plan by the end of the month, stating, "The pattern of separation by sex is a long established one in America and a system widely and generally accepted until the last decade. Despite this history, it seems clear to us that the Commonwealth of Virginia may not now deny to women, on the basis of sex, educational opportunities at the Charlottesville campus that are not afforded in other institutions operated by the state."[50]

UVA was on its way to becoming a coeducational institution. The BOV began the process of preparing for and accepting the first undergraduate class of women. They acted quickly, creating a plan in two days. The plan indicated that the next two years would be transition years, with women accepted in limited numbers in addition to men.[51] UVA would admit 450 women in the fall of 1970—350 first-year students and 100 transfers; and 550 in the fall of 1971—450 first-year students and 100 transfers.

Much of what has been written indicates full coeducation began in 1970, but that isn't totally accurate. It was the beginning of full coeducation. Full coeducation wouldn't occur, truly, until 1975, when the first class of women who entered would take their place in a university where all men and women were admitted on equal footing. Gender-blind admissions began with the class admitted in 1972. The university student population would not be fully coed until the fall of 1975, after the two restricted classes of women had graduated. The admissions practices to select the student population, at that juncture, would be free of the last vestiges of institutional gender discrimination.

This was the plan presented in Mannix's Minority Report. UVA's administration would continue to say that they had already made the commitment to coeducation before the lawsuit. President Shannon stated, "The ACLU and a number of people who were urging coeducation, of course, took the position that only by legal action had the University been brought kicking and screaming into the twentieth century, and it is true that we were required to admit [two of the four women filing the suit] without any conditions as to their relationship to the University a year before the Board had proposed to. On the other hand, the Board had of its own volition . . . made a genuine commitment to coeducation before any suit. But the waters of the University's action were muddied just a little bit that way."[52]

At a hearing the following December, the ACLU attorneys would attempt to get the court to rule in favor of all women, to apply *Brown v. Board of Education* to all Virginia schools of higher education, and to award the plaintiffs' damages. The court ruled against them on all three counts.

A Student's Perspective

In the spring of 1969, word of UVA's plans to coeducate had already spread on Grounds. Two years before my class arrived, my now husband, Larry, was offered a basketball scholarship at UVA. He remembers during his recruiting trip that faculty and students told him the school would be going coed in the fall of 1970. "I had gone to an all-boys Catholic high school in New York City and I really didn't want to go to a college that was all male," he said. "But in talking to the coaches and my brother Bill, who was already a student and basketball player there, everyone emphasized the fact that the school was going to go coed my second year, and I was excited for that." That, along with the university's brand-new Department of Environmental Sciences clinched his decision to attend. During Larry's first year, UVA was still all-male, and then in his second year, our class of women arrived, giving him a unique vantage point to the school's evolution.

Regardless of whether President Shannon was right and UVA was headed toward coeducation on its own, the court had mandated that women be admitted to the College of Arts and Sciences as undergraduates.

Now, to make it happen.

THREE

THE FIRST CADRE OF WOMEN

> Pressure is a privilege. It only comes to those who earn it.
> —Billie Jean King

ERNIE ERN, DEAN OF admissions, swung into action. Like me, other women had applied to UVA in 1969 not knowing that it was all-male at the time. Our applications were forwarded to Mary Washington College, the official women's college of UVA. Ern's first step after the BOV decision was to retrieve those forwarded applications and consider them for admission to UVA. Representatives from UVA also traveled to Mary Washington to recruit transfer students. Karen Wester Marcus (Education, '71; M.Ed., '72), a third-year student at UVA who had transferred from Mary Washington the previous summer, was a member of the Transition Committee. She remembers driving to her former school with Dean Mary Whitney to speak with women who had expressed interest in attending UVA. Transferring to UVA in the third and fourth years was a practice that was familiar to both institutions; however, previously transfers were primarily, if not exclusively, nursing and education students. This time, UVA was seeking one hundred additional transfer students to be admitted to the college as undergraduates. There appears to have been an attempt to also recruit second-year students, although enrollment figures indicate that only three women transferred as second-year students.

The exact numbers of women who transferred from Mary Washington, or any other institution for that matter, is information that is not available. Similarly, the registrar's office could not provide the exact number or the names of the first-year women admitted in 1970 to the College of Arts and Sciences. What is known for sure, though, is that after the October 1969 Board of Visitors decision to admit women, Ern and his team moved quickly to enroll approximately 367 first-year women and approximately 301 additional female upper-class transfers to the college in 1970. The estimated 367 first-year women were reported as having accepted and enrolled in the university as documented by Dean Ern in a report to the State Council of Higher Education for Virginia dated October 26, 1970 (and updated with a correction on November 4, 1970).

Women Apply in Large Numbers

The decision to coeducate UVA was made at a time during the year when many high school students had already applied to college, and if they had opted to partake in the early decision or early action process, a strategy employed by colleges since the 1950s to "lock in" incoming freshmen, they may have already committed to another college or university. This, then, already eliminated many potential applicants. But for those women who were able to apply after it became clear UVA would accept female first-year students in 1970, a surprising number of women indicated that their high school guidance counselors were not encouraging when they said they were going to apply.

It was reported that on numerous occasions counselors would tell interested female applicants that they were unlikely to be accepted, a common message being that they were "not good enough to go" or "not smart enough." And then, even after we were admitted, there were some men on campus who would echo these ideas, telling us when we took our place in UVA's classrooms that we were not good enough or smart enough to be there. Several classmates indicated they were even dissuaded from applying to UVA by their high school teachers or by older brothers; some reported being counseled not to attend by mothers who believed the culture would not be conducive to a female receiving a good education. Conversely, many of us were encouraged to apply and attend by parents, teachers, counselors, and administrators in our high schools. Susan (Susie) Clements Kiely (Arts and Sciences, '74) shared with me, "Once the decision was made to admit females, I had the full support of my teachers, counselor, and parents. And once I was accepted, everyone was happy and excited for me."

Some classmates from Virginia indicated that their parents, who had been entertaining the possibility of supporting them at an out-of-state or Ivy League college, changed their minds when they realized their daughters could get a quality education at UVA for a lot less money. In 1970, according to the National Center for Education Statistics, the average in-state tuition in the United States was about $350. In-state tuition at UVA for the 1970–71 school year was $484, while out-of-state tuition for that same period was $1,069. Although the in-state tuition was higher than the national average, this was still considered by many a bargain, given UVA's academic reputation. Several members of our class mentioned that UVA was not their first choice. Others indicated that their mothers were strong proponents of them attending UVA, sensing the historical importance of attending with the first class of undergraduate women, and believing that the positives would outweigh the potential negatives.

In Louise Robertson's 1986 study, "Modest Pioneers," she reported that the primary reason women gave for choosing to attend UVA was the academic reputation, followed by the cost, the opportunity to be among the first female students attending UVA's undergraduate College of Arts and Sciences, and the beauty of the Grounds and surrounding area. These reasons mirror what I found in my interviews thirty-five years later.

One woman I spoke with recalled that she knew several guys from high school who were at UVA, and they told her it was a great place to study and also have a fun social life. Another classmate shared that she loved the famous writer and former UVA student Edgar Allan Poe. He was her favorite writer, and when she saw his room on The Range, housing that is now used for some UVA graduate students, it sealed the deal. One student had a brother at UVA, and another said it was close enough to her home that she could get back on weekends if she wanted, or if she got homesick. A few women were not that excited about going; it really wasn't their first choice. But for family, financial, or other reasons, it was where they ended up.

"My dad insisted I apply," recalls Nancy Westcott (Arts and Sciences, '74). "I was a typical teenager and I cried because I knew [the coeducation case] was still in the courts and I wasn't sure we could attend. I thought it was pointless, but I rallied."

Paulette Jones Morant (Arts and Sciences, '74), one of the approximately thirty-five Black women in our class, shared that her mother was the catalyst for her application to UVA. Her parents, both educators, suggested that she apply. Paulette was somewhat hesitant, knowing that two of her friends and stellar leaders in her high school, Larry Sabato and Wyatt Andrews, were already committed to UVA. Paulette recalls, "My mother reminded me to hold myself accountable and to concentrate on my own talents. Confidence was a trait in continuous development." Thankfully, Paulette's mother encouraged her to apply, telling her not to be deterred.

In 2020, the UVA Alumni Association launched the ReTold initiative to celebrate the contributions of women and commemorate both the one hundredth anniversary of women's admission to graduate and professional schools in 1920 and the fiftieth anniversary of women's admission to the undergraduate programs in the College of Arts and Sciences. As part of the initiative, a series of webinars was conducted focusing on different aspects of the experiences of women at UVA. During one, "Women of the Class of 1974," which was moderated by Barbara Savage, panelists Beverly Agee Burton, Joan Kennedy, and Mary Bland Love discussed the admissions process.

Mary Bland Love (Arts and Sciences, '74), recalled, "I was in high school in Northern Virginia when my counselor suggested I apply to UVA because they were taking women. When I mentioned the idea to my mother, she was horrified. She had dated at UVA for the four years she was at Randolph Macon and had been Easter's Queen and she thought the whole place was very rough for a lady. But I applied and I got in. [When] I came down to get a look at things, I met Mary Whitney [UVA's dean of women], who at the time had an office on Poe Alley. She was very discouraging—she said it was a very difficult place for women and there had to be a suit to get us in. . . . So of course that convinced me that I should go."

Beverly Agee Burton (Arts and Sciences, '74), a Black woman in our class, explained her admission process in the same webinar:

Three hundred sixty-seven first-year women enrolled and started classes in September 1970. (1971 *Corks and Curls*)

My experience was totally different. I have been fond of saying that I got into UVA because of racism, but in thinking about it, I think I got into UVA in spite of racism. In high school, we had a college-bound track, and there were only two Black students in it [including me]. My guidance counselor did not share any information with me about going to college, never talked to me about going to college, never suggested that I would want to go [on a] tour, never suggested that I apply. . . . I had no idea that you had to take a test to get into college [she said, laughing].

One of my white friends, who is actually a member of the class, she and a group of people were talking one day about going to college and about going to UVA. I was asked, "Well, did you apply to UVA, Bev?" And I said, "No, why should I?" And, so, to make the long story short, when she learned that I had no information about going to college, had never been on a tour of any college, had never discussed with my guidance counselor any aspect of college, she was determined to get me into UVA. So, she got me an application and she actually paid the application fee. I didn't even know about programs like Upward Bound, who for first generation African Americans or people from poverty-stricken backgrounds was available to help you understand the [college entrance] process. . . . She actually paid the fees and paid for me to take the SAT because my parents were so poor. Most days I went to school, I didn't even have lunch money. So, I applied to one school, and I got in. [. . .] Then, one day, we were still in school, and we were walking down the hallway and this group of friends that I hung out with in my class started running toward the guidance counselor and they said, "Oh, we got in! We got in! We got in to UVA! All of us got in!" And [my friend] said, "And Bev got in too!" And my guidance counselor looked at me and said, "Well how on Earth did you ever manage that?" And that has lived with me and inspired me to be successful, in spite of anybody, actually, to this day.

Joan Kennedy (Architecture, '74) recalls,

I was seventeen years old, and unlike Mary Bland, had never laid eyes on the University of Virginia until I arrived on my first day. I was in Catholic school where the ratio of girls to boys was like three girls for every boy, and so, all of a sudden, to have those odds changed when I arrived here, [that was] really different for me. And, also . . . I was in architecture school. In retrospect though, I have come to understand that [being in the first class of women] was a very significant event. . . . We were the first foot in the door . . . we were a little piece of a big movement.

What Admissions Officers Were Looking For

There has always been keen interest in how this first cadre was selected—especially by those of us who are part of it. Giovana de Oliveira (Arts and Sciences, '21) spoke with Dean Ern and his wife, Petie, about this very topic on her podcast *Gritty Women,* a four-part examination of coeducation at UVA that was first broadcast in 2021. She asked him, as did I a year later, "What were you looking for in the women who would be in the first class of undergraduates?" He has been remarkably consistent in his responses over the years. He stated that he and his team were looking for exemplary applicants who were tenacious and well-rounded, who had strong academic backgrounds, and who were involved in leadership roles in their high schools. Most importantly, he said, the women he admitted were proven survivors "and full of grit."

The American Psychological Association defines "grit" as "a personality trait characterized by perseverance and passion for achieving long-term goals. Grit entails working strenuously to overcome challenges and maintaining effort and interest over time despite failures, adversities, and plateaus in progress. Recent studies suggest this trait may be more relevant than intelligence in determining a person's high achievement. For example, grit may be particularly important to accomplishing an especially complex task when there is a strong temptation to give up altogether."[1] Psychologist Angela Duckworth, author of *Grit: The Power of Passion and Perseverance,* has studied this concept extensively, developing a scale to allow a person to determine their level of grit.[2] Her research supports the idea that grit is a much more important quality in achieving success than talent. When I first heard the term used to describe our class, it seemed too rough and even seamy, but when defined this way, it feels apropos. We were plucky. We had to be.

In 1970, Annette Gibbs was hired as the new associate dean of student affairs, and while she was not on Grounds during the admissions process, she was in contact with the administration in the spring. As for what the university was looking for in ideal students, she said there was a concerted effort to enroll women who were "balanced" and "not only excelled in academics but who had personal goals and were involved in extracurricular activities."

My husband, Larry, remembers, "Before you and the other women came, some people thought it was going to be a very academic, bookish group—that you'd be women who studied all the time. But we were very pleasantly surprised. You all were an outstanding group of people—interesting, fun, and smart. Most of the women seemed strong and competent academically and socially, and you just seemed to fit in and thrive."

As Dean Gibbs noted in her oral history, there was some concern expressed that the women applying, especially out-of-state women, would be "radical feminists." One researcher indicated a marked divide among the women from New York and New Jersey, who he said were more liberal than the in-state women. He wrote that the women from northern Virginia, an area made up of several counties close to Washington, D.C., were a cross between the two camps. However, women surveyed for earlier studies and those who responded to my questions did not indicate a big divide. For the most part, the mix of women I met at UVA and have talked with for this book seems to include a cross-section of interests, political beliefs, and religions.

Wyatt Andrews (Arts and Sciences, '74), a classmate, former CBS correspondent, and former media professor at UVA, suggested that the success of the first class of women was in no small part attributable to Dean Ern's admission process. "I told him when I last saw him," Andrews said, "'One of the reasons everything went so well is you did such a great job selecting the women in our class.'"

Margaret Ann (Ann) Brown (Arts and Sciences, '74; Law, '77) echoed that feeling. A "very important reason for the success of coeducation was the real screen that Ernie Ern used in choosing us. He was looking for women he thought not only could do the academic work, but who he thought could get very engaged in student life."

According to the enrollment numbers sent to the state by the admissions office, in-state women comprised approximately 83 percent of the first-year women in 1970, and according to my analysis, almost 50 percent of the in-state women came from northern Virginia communities. The university's Office of Institutional Research and Analytics reported that in 1970 a total of 121 undergraduate students who self-identified as Black entered the university. Of the total, 89 students entered the College of Arts and Sciences, 19 registered in engineering, and the remainder enrolled in architecture, education, and nursing. This was a significant increase in Black student enrollment from previous years. Black undergraduate student enrollment in 1968 and 1969 was 22 and 42, respectively.

There are no data available that would indicate with any certainty the numbers of Black applicants, nor how many men versus women were accepted and enrolled. The *Cavalier Daily*, however, reported that 70 Black women applied for spots in the first-year class, and based on my research, it appears about 35 enrolled. With the 1970 class, not only did the university advance in terms of gender equity, but it also took important initial steps toward racial equity, with Black women making up approximately 10 percent of the women in the class. The university's Office of Institutional Research and Analytics reported that in 1970, there were 89 Black students in the College of Arts and Sciences; therefore, the estimated 35

Black women in the first class of women comprised approximately 39 percent of the Black students in the college. But if the numbers reported by the *Cavalier Daily* are accurate, Black students comprised only 3.1 percent of the entire first-year class.

Transition Committee

In December 1969, the Student Council proposed that a committee be formed to identify potential needs of the women who would be arriving the following September and make recommendations. In the February 20, 1970, issue of the *Cavalier Daily*, it was reported that a "special committee of University students, faculty, and staff members had three female undergraduates added to its ranks to help plan for the admission of women to the College of Arts and Sciences next fall," but only after several of the committee members complained that there were only two female members on the original committee. Originally established as a subcommittee, but eventually elevated to a special committee, its purpose was to "advise the Vice President for Student Affairs and recommend ways to assist in the smooth transition of co-education in the College."

In what might seem, in retrospect, like a gendered decision, the committee was chaired by Ralph Cherry, an education professor and former dean of the School of Education. No female administrators or faculty were members of the first or subsequent committees. In the fall 2020 issue of *Virginia Magazine*, UVA's alumni publication, the committee is deemed a "blue-ribbon committee." But what work it might have accomplished was essentially halted once May hit, and students on college campuses around the country began a wave of concerted protests. As Kevin Mannix (Arts and Sciences, '71; Law, '74) recalls, "It was all about the Student Strike from that point on."

University Growth Plan Supported

The university leadership had high aspirations and plans for UVA. They saw the school becoming a premier university and the additional women as providing a natural path to grow the overall student population. The administration planned to use this increase in enrollment to lobby Virginia lawmakers for additional funds. The larger student body would be used as a means for the university to expand and upgrade buildings and facilities. In the years following 1970, this was considered a desirable outcome of coeducation, another feather in the university's cap, so to speak, and helped counteract the residual dissatisfaction from the lawsuit. In fact, some administrators, while balking at the forced inclusion of women by a court decision, recognized that the additional women and the larger applicant pool ensured the quality of students and the growth needed to achieve goals set by President Shannon and the BOV.

There was, however, another concern: the university had a deep and strong alumni base who showed their support with gifts of their time, talent, and—money. Letters from alumni during the pivotal years of committee work and communications concerning coeducation showed that some alumni planned to stop their donations, should the university accept women. The university relied on gifts to fund new programs, grants, and construction, as well as to sustain ongoing priorities. Budgets are built, in part, by including pledges, and when donors, alumni, and others cancel planned giving, it can have a significant impact.

UVA certainly wasn't alone in their concerns about losing alumni donations after coeducation. Laura Brodie, in her book *Breaking Out: VMI and the Coming of Women*, about the coeducation of Virginia Military Institute in 1997, indicated that the school

> had been bracing for a drop in financial support. Prior to their Board of Visitors' decision to admit women, VMI's alumni agencies had polled several colleges, including Dartmouth, the University of Virginia, the Naval Academy, and Princeton, asking how coeducation had impacted alumni giving. In each case, the school had experienced a substantial drop in donations that lasted from four to five years after the admission of women. Princeton officials informed VMI that their alumni giving had plummeted by 30 percent in their early years of coeducation. Most of these schools, however, had chosen to admit women, alienating alumni who disagreed with the decision. In VMI's case, the vast majority of alumni felt that their alma mater had fought the good fight, taking their cause all the way to the US Supreme

Court, and doing all that it could to remain single-sex. They were willing to stick by their school as it faced a task that it had not invited.³

Alternatively, during the planning process, one UVA administrator suggested that a number of men who had attended UVA planned to send their daughters to their alma mater. This statement might have been crafted to placate alumni, but the administration did indicate that a sizable number of applicants for the first class of women were legacies, and although there are no available data to determine how many alumni's daughters enrolled, there is indication that it was significant.

Gibbs, in a 1991 oral history interview, stated, "Over the first four years I could visibly see the resistance breaking down among the alumni, because many of the alumni had daughters who were here. And when those daughters began educating their fathers to the merits of coeducation at their father's alma mater, that resistance did back away." While there were certainly women who entered in 1970 and the years soon after whose fathers attended UVA, it is unclear exactly how many.

Patriarchal Culture Emanates from the Top

While the majority of faculty responses to the "need to coeducate" were overwhelmingly supportive, there was little question that the faculty remained a male-dominant—and, in some, if not most, departments, a male-only—cadre. There were very limited numbers of female professors, and the majority of women faculty were, as one might expect at that time, in the School of Education and School of Nursing. Some women were recruited to join the faculty over the summer between the decision to admit women and our arrival, but many were hired as adjunct instructors.

The university's patriarchal leanings ran all the way back to Jefferson. As Jon Meacham said in his book *Thomas Jefferson*, "Inspired by his own father's example, he long sought to play the part of a patriarch, accepting— even embracing—the accompanying burdens of responsibility."⁴

Leo Damrosch, Ernest Bernbaum Research Professor of Literature, Emeritus, at Harvard, was a young assistant professor in UVA's English department during the early coeducation years. He remembers a "clubby"

UNIVERSITY OF VIRGINIA ADMINISTRATION

Edgar Finley Shannon, Jr., A.B., A.M., D.Phil. (Oxon.), Litt.D., LL.D., D.Hum. / *President of the University*
Edwin M. Crawford, B.S. / *Vice President for Public Affairs*
Frank Loucks Hereford, B.A., Ph.D. / *Vice President and Provost of the University*
Thomas Harrison Hunter, M.D. / *Vice President for Medical Affairs*
Vincent A. Shea, B.A., M.A. / *Vice President for Business and Finance*
D. Alan Williams, B.A., M.A., Ph.D. / *Vice President for Student Affairs*
Charles Cortez Abbott, A.B., A.M., Ph.D. / *Dean of the Graduate School of Business Administration*
Joseph Norwood Bosserman, B.S. in Arch., M.F.A. / *Dean of the School of Architecture*
Robert T. Caneveri, B.Ed., M.Ed. / *Dean of Students*
Irby Bruce Cauthen, Jr., B.A., M.A., Ph.D. / *Dean of the College of Arts and Sciences*
Kenneth Raymond Crispell, B.S., M.D. / *Dean of the School of Medicine*
Frederick R. Cyphert, B.S., M.A., Ed.D. / *Dean of the School of Education*
Andre Charles dePorry, B.S.F.S. / *Dean of the School of General Studies*
Ernest H. Ern, B.S., M.S., Ph.D. / *Dean of Admissions*
Frank Sanford Kaulback, Jr., B.S., M.A., Ph.D. / *Dean of the McIntire School of Commerce*
Mary M. Lohr, B.S.N.Ed., M.A., Ed.D. / *Dean of the School of Nursing*
Monrad G. Paulsen, A.B., J.D. / *Dean of the School of Law*
Lawrence Reginald Quarles, B.S.E., Ph.D. / *Dean of the School of Engineering and Applied Science*
David A. Shannon, B.S., M.A., Ph.D. / *Dean of the Faculty of Arts and Sciences*
Walter Dexter Whitehead, Jr., B.S., M.S., Ph.D. / *Dean of the Graduate School of Arts and Sciences*

The University of Virginia's administration in September 1970. (*The Colonnade*, Office of the Registrar, September 1970; author's collection) atmosphere in the department, with older professors who saw themselves in a "fatherly" role. There were no tenured female faculty members in the department. The department was just beginning to hire female professors at the time—although not promoting them. Damrosch said the admission of women created the impetus for the university to move beyond a "Gentlemen's school where students drank a lot" into a much more vital and academic university. He stated that his "very best students were women," a nod to some of my classmates, including Nancy Forbes (Arts and Sciences, '74), who introduced us, virtually, before her sudden and untimely death in December 2020.

The Colonnade, a pamphlet included with the information in the orientation packets we received in September 1970, listed on the inside cover twenty University of Virginia administrators, among them one woman, the dean of the School of Nursing.[5] If we thought our entry would change the fundamental operations of the university, this, along with other orientation materials, would quickly squash that notion. This topic is explored further in the next few chapters.

Men Are Challenged "To Do Better"

In an April 25, 1970, editorial in the *Cavalier Daily* entitled "Feminine Attitudes," the authors expressed pleasure in the decision by the oldest honor society at UVA, the Raven Society, to admit women, after sixty-six years of exclusive male membership. "What made that decision especially pleasing was that the Raven Society went ahead and chose several women for membership, instead of waiting several years," they wrote.

> Certainly, the University community has come a long way in accepting the presence of women here. In 1934, this column contained an editorial which stated: "A university is for learning and discussion, but when it is coeducational it becomes a place for playing and for love." The editorial concluded with the following words about the incoming women students: "We maintain that their coming here in ever increasing numbers bodes no good for the University. Great universities are not coeducational. The big

machine-age university, such as those of the far south and middle west, would not be so despised by certain groups of intelligentsias, if they were not handicapped by the unfortunate atmosphere created by the presence of both male and female students. If Virginia draws more coeds, and if the lure and lilt of the Lawn gives way to the love-making atmosphere of the midwestern campus, we advocate a second Rotunda fire and the deletion of the last phrase, 'founder of the University of Virginia,' from Jefferson's epitaph."

The 1970 editorial continues, "The problem is a most difficult one to correct. Rules can be changed. But can the attitude of the large minority of students be changed so easily? This newspaper certainly has a strong record of male chauvinism." The editorial concludes:

> The largest percentage of male chauvinists here are the undergraduate population. With the admission of women these young men, who usually only meet the opposite sex under artificial conditions, will see girls doing the same work they are and facing similar problems. Many of next year's entering class will be living in dormitories with members of the opposite sex a floor or two above or below them. Once the Virginia Gentleman discovers that his fellow female student is indeed a human being he will, we pray, begin treating her like one.[6]

Coeducation Takes a Back Seat

Of course, the attitudes of the male faculty and students who opposed the admission of women did not change automatically with the October 1969 BOV policy decision, but during the spring of 1970, issues related to the war in Vietnam and the invasion of Cambodia became the paramount concern on the Grounds. Protests were held at more than seven hundred university and college campuses around the country, including at UVA. By the end of April 1970, American troops would invade Cambodia. For the many Americans who opposed the Vietnam War, this was a clear expansion of the war, the antithesis of the de-escalation and troop withdrawal promised by the Nixon administration. On May 4, four unarmed students protesting the war were shot and killed by Ohio National Guardsmen on the campus of Kent State University. Students across the nation mobilized to show their outrage, and nothing else mattered in that moment. Other conversations, including those around coeducation, ceased, replaced by the call for a student strike. University leadership, paying close attention to what was happening at schools to the north, knew the unrest would end up in Charlottesville, and in May 1970, UVA student leaders were beginning to organize protests.

My husband, Larry, who was a first-year student at the time, says, "All I remember anyone thinking about and being concerned with that spring was the war and the draft. All the men had had to sign up at the draft office when we turned 18, and we knew that after college there was a chance we would be drafted into the army. There was a lot going on, and it was a real time of unrest."

It didn't surprise anyone that Kent State was the match that ignited the powder keg. The horror of that day cannot be overstated. The scene of National Guardsmen firing into a crowd of students, and the images of dead and bleeding students is one that most Americans alive then have seared in their memories. College students at that time had lived through the 1960s, a time of enormous social turmoil as the country grappled with segregation, racism, assassinations, and the seemingly never-ending war in Vietnam. The emotional toll the Vietnam War was taking on Americans who watched it play out live on television each night, and the toll on the young soldiers and soldiers' families, was dizzying. These years were incredibly concentrated periods of both tragedy and positive change. This was the backdrop for the first class of women preparing to enter the University of Virginia.

Changing of the Guard

As mentioned in the previous chapter, Dean of Women Mary Whitney left UVA at the end of June 1970. She worked that winter and spring on issues related to facilities and housing. On March 23, 1970, she sent a letter to those of us who had been admitted about prospective dorm assignments and explained the setup of the coeducational dorms. The letter read, in part, "The assignment of first year men and women to the self-contained suites either in the separate women's building or the combined buildings will be carried out on a random basis. However, first year men and women will not be assigned to suites on the same floor in any of the combined buildings."[7] It appears that in her final months at the university she was doing some recruiting for transfer students. She also sent a memo to D. Alan Williams, vice president of student affairs, regarding a question about allowing the one sorority on Grounds to rush. She expressed concern that based on past practices she doubted opportunities would be extended to Black women, presuming some were admitted. Her statement implies a lack of knowledge about the incoming class of women, suggesting that she was not involved in admissions decisions, or if she were, it was peripheral, at most.

Annette Gibbs began July 1 as the associate dean of students, and her responsibilities would include advising male students as well as female students. But as she stated in an oral history conducted in November 1991, she came "to the University for the purpose of implementing coeducation."[8]

"At the time I was at Florida State completing my doctorate," she said. "I had no intentions of coming to the University of Virginia. I had been a Dean of Students and then a Vice President for Student Affairs at an institution of about 6,500 students, which, at the time, really wasn't much smaller than UVA. . . . I did come to coeducate, and it took us, I would say, about two years to really do it."

As mentioned earlier, though Annette Gibbs was not officially on staff or in Charlottesville until July 1, she was in contact with and advising President Shannon and Dean Ern throughout the spring of 1970. She said she weighed in on admissions issues and other decisions that were made. She made several trips to Charlottesville prior to officially beginning her job, and just as Whitney had, Gibbs voiced her concerns about lighting and security issues. After arriving in July, she made safety as well as the construction and renovation of women's bathrooms a priority.

Ready or Not

Later that winter and into the spring, incoming female students would visit UVA, and some families, especially those who lived in cities not far from Grounds, would make a day trip to Charlottesville during the summer of 1970. My father, sister, and I drove nine hours in the family station wagon to visit on my spring break, leaving behind my home, where it was still cold and snowy, and arriving in Charlottesville to a glorious sunny spring day. There is little question that the beauty of the Grounds and surrounding countryside captivated me and helped inform my decision to attend. So, too, did the student my sister and I met on the steps of the Rotunda as we were hunting for the admissions office. He personally delivered us to Dean Ern's office, waving my acceptance letter in his hand and exclaiming to everyone in the office, "Dean Ern, this is Gail Burrell and her sister, Linda, from Michigan. Gail is the first girl I've ever met to be accepted to UVA!"

Talk about feeling special! How was I to say no to that?

FOUR

BY GOD, I THINK THEY'RE HERE...

> No one can make you feel inferior without your consent.
> —Eleanor Roosevelt

WE ARRIVED ON SATURDAY and Sunday in mid-September, stuffed in sedans, station wagons, and the occasional VW beetle. Most of the first-year women didn't have far to travel. There were 367 of us in all, according to Dean Ern's report. Eighty-three percent of the first-year women were from Virginia, and 50 percent of those were from the communities of northern Virginia. My classmate Alarie Tennille (Arts and Sciences, '74) wrote about those first heady days in her poem "Summer 1970, The University of Virginia Opens to Women in the Fall," which was first published in the *Southern Women's Review*:

> Mama calls me a pioneer. I call
> me a student—tagging along
> after my older brother like always,
> ignoring his taunts. *You can't
> come here.* Somehow I knew
> I would.
>
> At thirteen, I fell in love
> with Thomas Jefferson's Rotunda

Newcomb Hall was, and still is, the main place for students to eat and the hub for activities. (1974 *Corks and Curls*)

and vistas of the Blue Ridge.
I'm not trying to make history,
just taking my place in it.

Brave? No, timid and half blind.
Every stranger and new school
scares me. That's life.
I don't know I'll need extra
courage. That will come later.

Almost all of us would live in the Alderman Road dorms, then called "the new dorms," which, except for Courtenay, Dunglison, and Fitzhugh, have since been rebuilt in a style more hall-like than the originals, which were designed as suites. The "old dorms" of our era, however, still house some of today's students. Male students would share space with us in Alderman Road—the two coeducational dorms housed men on the lower floors and women on the upper. Men also lived in the dorms on McCormick Road, which were closer to classroom buildings, and Newcomb Hall, which functioned as the student union building and housed the cafeteria, "Mama Newks," where students on "contract," or the meal plan, ate during the week.

Here We Come

Women made up just 18 percent of the class that first year.[1] In the years since, a different percentage has been erroneously reported, which I think either conflates the number of female first-year students with transfer students or is the result of a simple math error. The 100 transfers called for in the court-approved plan would be primarily third-year students and would be in addition to the transfers typically admitted to the Schools of Education and Nursing. The total number of female transfer students in the second-, third-, and fourth-year classes was 301, and these new upperclass students would combine with women already attending.

The number of first-year and transfer women to be admitted was agreed to in the court-approved plan, although the number admitted would exceed the agreement. A commitment was also made not to displace any qualified male students, a tenet of the recommendation made by the administration and approved by the BOV. All of this meant that the following several years saw significantly increased enrollments. As discussed in the next chapter, this would create housing shortages, parking challenges, and concern about the growth of the university. Dean Ern's report with complete 1970 enrollment numbers makes this evident; a table documenting total applications and enrollment for fall 1970 (including first-time and transfer first-year students, as well as transfer second-, third-, and fourth-year students) confirms that 2,399 first-time and transfer students were enrolled (1,577 in-state and 822 out-of-state), of which 1,731 were men and 668 were women.

Those first days, we met our roommate and suitemates and figured out how to arrange our room. I was assigned to a suite on the second floor of Maupin, a dorm built on a hill that overlooked a grassy bowl-like area, the Glass Hat snack bar, and other dorms. In the distance were Scott Stadium (football) and glimpses of the Blue Ridge Mountains. I arrived with a footlocker that to my dismay did not, in fact, fit under my bed, a gray IBM Selectric typewriter that my dad had won playing craps, an eight-track player, and not much else. I would quickly come to find out that having an electric typewriter was a rarity and in high demand. I often lent it to my suitemates, and since I had taken a typing class the summer before eighth grade and was a proficient typist, I later used this skill to make a few bucks by typing my male classmates' papers.

Susan Byers Tribble (Arts and Sciences, '74) remembers, "From the second I arrived at UVA, I felt at home, which was really astounding considering I was a shy and not particularly sociable person. I was in a suite with wonderful, fun women, most of whom got along quite well with each other."

Diane Kirchner Knetzger (Arts and Sciences, '74) recalls, "I was swept up in the excitement and the energy of the experience, and I loved UVA from the start."

On Display

As soon as we stepped on campus, many of us had a sense of being watched or, as one classmate described it, "on display." Karen Brainard (Nursing, '74) remembers lining up to pick up her room key and there being a gauntlet of men she had to walk through. Threading our way through throngs of men would become the norm for the next week. Groups of men would stand on stairs and outside suites on the balconies. Carolyn Welch Brumbaugh (Arts and Sciences, '74) remembers "hordes of college men standing outside the women's dorms. I had to walk through them every time I went to class or to eat. That was very distressing to a shy first-year."

Even among first-years, a term we would soon learn if we didn't know UVA-speak already, we were outnumbered more than four to one. That ratio would become significantly more lopsided when the upperclassmen arrived later in the week. Many of us in that first cohort had no idea that we would comprise such a small portion of the class. We were chagrined to hear that there were some alumni who claimed that our only motivation for attending UVA was because the odds were in our favor of "snagging a husband."

Male students gathered outside the dorms, helping unload cars and carry footlockers and suitcases up the flights of stairs. Weary and often emotionally drained parents were thankful for the help, and the young men used the opportunity to introduce themselves to their new classmates. As we said our good-byes to our parents, some who were off to a Sunday parent meeting, others who were leaving for home, the newness and excitement turned to anxiety. Some of us had never shared a room with another person and, until then, had maintained a certain amount of privacy. The urinals and open showers in our dorms were obvious relics of the recent male occupants. Some women put flowers in the urinals, a constant reminder that we had entered what had formerly been a male world.

Groups of men also began floating from suite to suite "looking for their old room," a line that quickly got old. "The bands of men invading the suites" were too much for some of us. They clearly had "come to look at the women," one classmate remarked. Many of the men wielded copies of *The First Year Directory of the Class of 1974*, often referred to as "the facebook," before Facebook was a thing, and it didn't take long to realize how the pictures we had sent for inclusion in this pamphlet were, and would continue to be, used.[2] Although I remember that our room doors locked, the suite door didn't, or if it did, it never seemed to be locked. Not even going into our rooms and closing the door stopped male students from knocking—and sometimes pounding—on our doors. The traffic continued, the men seemingly undeterred by our signals, both subtle and overt. Annette Gibbs remembered, "Men would hang around—in fact, they would jump off the rafters and hang around the balconies of the Alderman Road dorms day and night. So, women had a lot of male companionship, but they didn't have real privacy among themselves and chances to go and [be by] themselves."[3]

From the very first evening, many of us remember the noise. It was warm, and the dorms were not air-conditioned, nor were there overhead fans. But opening windows meant a barrage of warring songs and the whoops of frisbee-playing men, often late into the night. We would find out that technically there were parietal hours during the week, designated times when men were allowed to visit, but in many suites they were ignored, and men staying overnight in dorm rooms became common. The circus-like atmosphere would become worse once the upperclassmen arrived later in the week.

One classmate commented, "[The upperclassmen] were more organized. They had the room numbers written down of women they had seen on the facebook, and it was clear they were comparing the picture to the real thing."

Nancy Forbes (Arts and Sciences, '74) noted that men came to our dorms to "check out the goods, looking for dating material. It was awkward and even humiliating as some women had multiple guys seeking them out, and others were being ignored or shunned. The message was: hey, if you're good looking and good date material, you'll have a successful social life here and be 'popular'—otherwise, no."

Tiring of all the attention, most of us learned to ignore the men outside our rooms. One classmate said, "Nothing stopped the men from hanging around, even when we told them to go away." Another classmate noted, "After the fourth or fifth guy went to the same room, we all knew who was considered the prettiest woman in our suite." Another commented, "They would use the facebook to invite women to mixers and parties, and I remember being especially offended when the Black women in our suite didn't get invitations."

There were some factions on campus who considered the first-year women to be snobby and arrogant. Other men labeled us "dogs." Frances Dickinson (Dickie) McMullan (Arts and Sciences, '74) remembers we were referred to as "UChicks," a label that differentiated us from "women from nearby girls' schools." It has been reported that we were also called "UBags," although no man I spoke with admitted to remembering, let alone using, any of these labels. Some men would later insist they were justified in continuing the age-old tradition of "going down the road" or "rolling" to all-girls' schools for dates, because either we wouldn't date them, or we weren't worth dating. This phase didn't last long, thankfully.

Convocation and Reception

In our orientation materials, there was a letter from President Shannon announcing the Monday convocation. When the evening arrived for the convocation, we walked together down Alderman Road, joining the men from McCormick Road dorms, past the gas station and Foods of All Nations on Ivy Road, and on to University Hall (U-Hall), en masse. Kathleen McGinn (Arts and Sciences, '74) said, "I don't remember being aware of how few women would be matriculating until I arrived at school in the Fall of 1970 and the whole class went to U-Hall for a speech from various deans and administrators. The girls were clearly outnumbered, though I don't remember being bothered or intimidated by that fact."

Shannon's letter also stated, "Later in the week, on Wednesday, 16 September, at 4:30 P.M., Mrs. Shannon and I will enjoy the opportunity of greeting you personally at a reception to be held at our home on Carr's Hill." The reception, a traditional tea held each year by the President and Mrs. Shannon, was a confusing mix of old U and new U, with female students from Sweet Briar, Mrs. Shannon's alma mater, pouring the tea.

The Sweet Briar students and their classmates would, along with women from the other area women's colleges, make another appearance several weeks later. They were many men's dates for Homecomings, with an s, another idiosyncratic UVA word, the first "big" weekend that included a football game and lots of parties. Many of the UVA women were left dateless. This was our first taste of being "popular" during the week and dateless on the weekend.

Suite Talks

Each suite was paired with a "sister suite" and shared a counselor, typically a transfer student in her third or fourth year. One classmate related that she had a male counselor, but that wasn't common. During Orientation Week, the two suites would come together for a "dorm talk" most evenings. Classmates remember a very awkward session on pregnancy, contraception, and abortion, with a two-page, back and front, legal-sized mimeographed paper on all these topics. These would be topics that women from our class, when becoming counselors or resident advisors (RAs) our second year, would tackle in more depth, greatly improving communication and information.

The presentation also included information about student health services. The services—or lack thereof—available to women at that time were unsettling, especially because, as we would find out, either by calling for an appointment or walking over to inquire about resources, there was no gynecologist on staff our first year. By the second year, one gynecologist was available just two afternoons a week, requiring months-long waits.

One classmate recalls a "talk" with their counselor about drugs. She remembers being particularly disconcerted by their advice, "to flush the drugs down the toilet" if campus security or the Charlottesville police showed up at the suite. This advice, while seemingly unnecessary for the students who weren't pot smokers or who didn't use illegal drugs, would foreshadow several drug raids or "busts" in the dorms both by campus and city police. Arrests were also made at off-Grounds housing and fraternity houses. The use of drugs, as well as drug-related arrests, would increase during our UVA years. In 1972, Dean of Students Robert Canevari threatened to cancel live concerts at U-Hall due to drug use. In an article in the September 28, 1972, *Cavalier Daily*, Canevari is quoted as saying, "I even heard of several girls who felt they had to leave because they feared getting high from the marijuana being smoked around them."

Another dorm session described UVA traditions and the language, or "UVA-speak," we would use as students. For example, as previously mentioned the campus was called "the Grounds," which at some point after we left changed to just "Grounds," and professors with a Ph.D. weren't called "Doctor," but "Mister." And, of course, we were not freshmen, we were "first-years." We would learn that students at other Virginia colleges thought UVA students' distinct lingo was evidence of our self-perceived elitism.

While these talks were intended as an ongoing part of dorm life, it appears they were more theoretical than a reality. A surprising number of classmates reported very little interaction with their counselors, and one noted that after Orientation Week she and her suitemates never saw their counselor again.

Honor Code

UVA has a unique, student-governed honor system that was established in 1842. Students commit not to lie, cheat, or steal on campus, in the surrounding community, and anytime they are representing the university. If accused of having committed an Honor Code violation, students are investigated, prosecuted, defended, and tried by their fellow students. Materials about the Honor Code were sent to incoming students over the summer, and it was also discussed during orientation. We would learn, if we didn't know already, that the Honor Code and the system of student self-governance was foundational to UVA. The fundamental belief that students would behave "honorably" undergirded every aspect of UVA life, from unattended purses on tables to unlocked dorm rooms to take-home tests and exams. It was so much a part of our existence at the university that it always felt shocking to see the telltale little black box in the *Cavalier Daily* announcing that someone had left the university because of an honor offense.

The dorm talk exclusively about the Honor Code was a long and detailed presentation from a member of the Honor Committee. Directly after, each of us was asked to sign a contract agreeing to abide by the code. An interesting and controversial tenet of the Honor Code was the fact that you were excused from the no-lying part of the code to illegally purchase or obtain alcohol. While this was long practiced, it was codified in writing in 1969.[4] There were some who found this to be the height of hypocrisy, and others that accepted the inevitability of this long-established Virginia Gentlemen tradition. At any rate, the exception was an indication of how prevalent underage drinking was in the fabric of a UVA student's life.

It should be noted that the Honor System and the Honor Code have been discussed, debated, litigated, and amended over the years. Many consider it to be foundational to the university and defend it vigorously. During our time there, a student who was accused of an Honor Code violation was considered guilty and expected to leave the Grounds. Subsequently, a hearing could be requested that would determine if a student would be reinstated. There were concerns, obviously, about the constitutionality of being "presumed guilty" and lack of due process and individual rights. A friend who was accused of an honor violation recounted that after the hearing and a "not guilty" verdict, the classmate who had accused him approached him and said, "Welcome back to the university."

Beer, Grain, and Pot

The entire first week after we arrived, there was a party, of sorts, in the grassy area between Maupin and Lile dorms, in suites, and in the halls of the old dorms. Some of us got our first taste of grain punch (made with high-proof grain alcohol), and others smoked our first college pot. Many chose not to participate in what was a noisy, seemingly drunken and stoned meet-and-greet.

Some women who had male friends from high school at UVA would travel in a group with other women to the rooms of men they knew from back home. These gatherings were reportedly more civilized. Some female counselors, friendly with a male counselor, introduced the women and men they were advising through informal "get-togethers." The student council sponsored some social events, including a first-year mixer at Newcomb Hall the weekend after classes started.

Registration at Memorial Gym

Once we arrived, every member of the first-year class received a time slot to go to Memorial Gym—the old fieldhouse used mainly for intramurals, pickup basketball games, and swimming—to register for our classes. This registration process was hot and long and very frustrating. One classmate said it was a "nightmare," and another called it "chaos."

For those of us who received a Thursday, late-afternoon registration slot, it was nothing short of a disaster. Classes started Friday morning, and by Thursday afternoon all the introductory classes were filled and had waiting lists. While we had received academic counseling, of sorts, earlier in the week from advisors, it proved to be almost meaningless because many of the classes that had been identified as a good "first" class for a possible major or area of interest were no longer available. All the classes that began later in the day were taken, especially the foreign language sections, and many of us were forced to register for early morning classes, knowing full well that *if* we made it to class—and that was a big *if*—we would certainly not be at our best. One classmate, the minority it seems, remembers registration fondly, writing about "the sunlight pouring through the tall windows of the gym."

In lieu of good options, many of us resorted to asking professors to admit us to upper-level classes for which we lacked the prerequisites. And conversely, after sitting through an upper-level class and feeling overwhelmed and out of our league, some of us begged professors of introductory classes to find room for us.

Physicals and the Dreaded Swimming Requirement

While there were certainly tears (note: my hand is raised here) and meltdowns and frustrations around the class registration process, many recall another vexing part of the start to the school year. Why, if we had physicals prior to arriving in Charlottesville, were we required to troop to the hospital, suite by suite, for yet another one? Many of us suspected these physicals were less about us and more about offering a practicum to UVA medical students. The experience of the physical was demeaning, as we sat in hospital gowns in long, not-even-close-to-private hallways, waiting for our exams. The one positive outcome of the physicals, it seemed, was that it bonded suitemates who made the trek to the hospital together.

The arrival of women had another unintended consequence—one for which we would find ourselves unexpectedly thanked, though we had done nothing to achieve it—the elimination of the swimming requirement. For years, although no one can tell me how long, UVA students would walk to Memorial Gym (Mem Gym), dive in the water, and swim a lap, thus "passing the swimming requirement." When we arrived, however, because there were not yet any locker rooms for women, the requirement was dropped and never reinstated. Lack of facilities also accounted for no physical education offerings for women our first year.

Navigating Grounds

During Orientation Week, we were given tours of Grounds and classroom buildings, but the reality of finding our way and getting to class on time didn't really sink in until classes started that Friday. This was an era when many classes still met on Fridays, which is not nearly as common today.

Mary McKeone Ellmore (Arts and Sciences, '74) recalls, "Finding my way around was crazy. It was at UVA I discovered I have NO sense of direction." Laura Wilson Small (Arts and Sciences, '74) said, "At the beginning of my first year, I remember walking into a class in Cabell Hall a few minutes late, after getting lost, and the professor stopped mid-sentence. The students, all male, turned around and silently stared at me. I found the closest seat and sat down as quickly as I could in hopes that everyone would stop staring."

It would become clear to us during the first week of classes that Alderman Road, where our dorms were located, was a long distance from most of our classrooms, and an even longer hike to anything in downtown Charlottesville and The Corner (a popular business district that abuts Grounds). For a while, the strip-style retail area Barracks Road was the only shopping spot, and it was more than three miles round-trip. The Corner shops, which had catered primarily to men for decades, would quickly adapt and begin offering some nice—though pricey—clothing for women. Kevin Mannix (Arts and Sciences, '71; Law, '74), recalls the student council operating a few buses our second semester. These buses ran mostly at night and primarily in response to women's concerns about safety and lighting. The bus schedule, though, was sporadic, and there weren't enough buses to encircle the Grounds. For the most part, we walked to class, to the library, and to eat. Essentially, we walked everywhere.

My first date with Larry (Arts and Sciences, '73) was in February 1971. We went to a party that he and his fellow teammates were throwing in the suite where many of the basketball players lived. At some point during the night, I wanted him to dance with me and was attempting to pull him up off the couch where he was sitting. I lost my balance, fell backward, and hurt my knee—badly. Though neither of us knew the extent of my injury then, he carried me up the stairs to my dorm that night. Early Sunday morning, I called my roommate's boyfriend who had a car, and he drove me to the emergency room, where scans indicated that I'd suffered tendon and ligament damage, but no break. Nonetheless, my leg was put in a cast from my ankle up to my thigh. When Larry came to see me the next day, my suitemates and I staged a "big reveal" covering my leg with a blanket that we dramatically removed.

"I thought it must be a prank," Larry said. "I didn't see how it could be real. I felt awful." Because my dorm was across the Grounds from most of my classes, the cast proved to be more than a little inconvenient. Thankfully, if we pushed the passenger seat all the way back in his tiny Volkswagen Beetle, I could fit in with my fully outstretched casted leg. It should be noted that this was nothing short of a miracle since I am 5′9½″ (or was) with a 36″ inseam! And so that's how our love story began, with Larry driving me to my classes whenever his class and basketball schedules would allow. I must say, upon reflection, that this is one example of when the university's hands-off approach with us first-year women didn't work so well. I don't recall even our dorm counselor providing any assistance in what would become a considerable challenge getting to class in a full-leg cast. Without buses, I remember being physically exhausted much of my second semester. I missed a lot of classes, and it took a couple of years before my GPA recovered.

I wasn't the only one who had health challenges our first year. Liz McLeod (Arts and Sciences, '74) recalls a very bad case of mononucleosis the first semester that made her miss many of her classes. "I was so scared that I would fall behind," she said, "but fortunately, much of the material covered, I had either touched on in high school or could read while recovering. My professors were kind about extending deadlines."

Personhood Is Our Right

As we settled into life at the university, we would learn a lot about ourselves, our world, and our ability to live apart from our parents and families. With newfound independence, we would even make a few adult decisions, navigating new relationships and new living situations. Some of us did a better job of acclimating than others.

There were also new academic demands. Most of the women who entered in 1970 went to highly rated high schools, secondary schools, or prep schools and took the most rigorous courses available to them. Most of us graduated at the top of our high school class. It was a rude awakening to discover in this new world that, in the words of a classmate, we were "average." Mary Payne VanderWall (Arts and Sciences, '74) said, "I just remember being overwhelmed with coursework. I could have benefited from having an actual faculty advisor." Women and men in our class would report that many classes were far too big and far too impersonal. We would discover that the writing we did in high school hadn't prepared us for the analytical critiques we were expected to produce. Some of us would be staggered by the amount of reading expected in every class. As an English major, I would have to "up my game," and reading speed, to get through my assignments.

Women were also aware that there were some classmates and especially upperclassmen who didn't think we had the intellectual "chops" to cut it at UVA. For some, this fed into our "imposter syndrome," heightening our sense of being in over our heads. For others, it was self-evident that admitting women would make UVA better and stronger. Anne Tausch (Arts and Sciences, '74) recalls, "Several 4th years came up to me and in essence said, 'no offense but women are going to diminish UVA.' I wasn't offended. I knew they were wrong."

In some cases, men had apparently made agreements with each other not to sit by women in classes. Rebecca (Bek) Sorrells Wheeler (Arts and Sciences, '74) said, "The reception we received was mixed—neither universally hostile, nor universally welcoming. Indeed, the unpredictability of our reception was one of the difficult aspects. One never knew what the reception would be. Many students and faculty were encouraging. Others were cold and aloof. Others were inappropriate."

A dorm counselor, in her fourth year, who had transferred from a college in New York the previous year, responded to the aforementioned 1996 alumnae survey, "Women were both welcomed and resented. The prejudice was subtle. I found most of it a bit ridiculous. Some students wore buttons which read, 'BBTOU—Bring Back the Old U.' Most students welcomed co-education, however. My husband [who was a fourth-year] felt his 1st and 2nd years at Virginia were very lonely. He disliked going on 'road trips' to the girls' school. Having women at the school was a positive change."[5]

We were also presented with the emotionally fraught argument from some male classmates that we were taking a space at the university that a man who was serving in Vietnam would have had if he had received the needed education deferment. This was awful to hear, even if it wasn't true. Women's enrollment the first two years was explicitly dictated to be in addition to men's enrollment.

We were told some professors also had their doubts. Michele Burpeau-Di Gregorio (Education, '74) stated, "There seemed to be some idea that we were an 'experiment' and if it didn't go well, we could ruin it for future women. Yet, I don't know that I really thought that it could be rolled back once it had started." According to Gibbs, the first-semester grade point average among women in the class was higher than that of the men. Some men were even heard complaining that they thought a "Gentleman's C" would be easy to obtain, only to have women wreck the curve.

Ken Elzinga, a professor of economics and a faculty member since 1967 who continues to teach today, speaks to coeducation as one of the most important changes during his tenure at the university. In an interview with Teresa Sullivan in 2021 he says:

> [Coeducation], obviously, was a big change in many ways, but one of the major ways was just [that] the academic quality of the College of Arts and Sciences took a leap. It took a real leap. Now, I have to be careful here. There were a lot of smart boys here when it was an all-male school. I met some incredibly smart kids, but the intensity of study in the classroom was not that high. There were smart kids who studied hard and showed themselves to be intellectually very talented, but there wasn't a lot of, I don't know . . . competition to really excel. And when the women came in, they were all top of their high school classes and they were here to learn and maybe to make a statement that they belonged here.[6]

The Paradox of Faculty Resistance

During the years that the committees explored coeducation, the faculty members were overwhelmingly supportive of the prospect. So, it might have come as a bit of a surprise that in the surveys and studies following our years on Grounds, women consistently reported that male professors, especially older ones, initially were one of the most difficult parts of our time at UVA.

Gibbs, in a 1991 oral history interview, stated:

> There was some faculty resistance. I told you there had been considerable faculty support for coeducation, and that's true. But there was also some counter faculty resistance, and it took a while for that. In the early years students said things like, "Oh, in all the lectures all the examples are about males. All the stories, all the illustrations, all the films, all the supporting documentations are male-focused." That's understandable. But I guess, what

is the old saying, that academicians change slowly? That was probably true relative to coeducation. It was not an overt, planned, belligerent resistance. Part of it was just natural. Part of it was just the nature of the beast.[7]

Burpeau-Di Gregorio remembers trying to stay under the radar. "The main advice that I strongly recall was that the full tenured professors would be the ones to worry about and to not sit up front to antagonize them," she said. "So, I recall trying to merge more into the crowd. Whether or not this is true, I don't know, but it was what I was told and it is part of my experience."

Elizabeth Gress Muenster Hunt (Arts and Sciences, '74) reported having a teaching assistant (TA) call her "'Mr. Gress,' all semester, and another TA would say, 'Very good, Miss Gress' whenever I answered a question. The tone of voice was just on the verge of sounding encouraging, or sarcastic—I could not decide which, but he sure didn't say that to the boys who answered questions."

One Black classmate indicated that when she and another female student arrived for their first class, the professor said to the class, "A few years back I had to get used to the Coloreds, now I guess I'll have to get used to the damn women."

Women remember being called on in every class by some instructors and never called on by others. One woman said, "I had one professor who hated me, and I never knew why."

As noted in an earlier chapter, Mary Whitney, prior to our arrival, surveyed women students and reported that they found their academic life very unsatisfactory.[8] Despite some bumps we encountered, I don't think Whitney's findings reflect the majority of our experiences. The responses I received related to coursework and the quality of instruction ran the gamut. For every story of difficulty, like those previously mentioned, there were other stories of respectful and professional behavior and treatment by professors, instructors, and TAs that appeared no different than the treatment of males.

Sharon Young Bailey (Arts and Sciences, '74) said, "I loved going to class. I majored in Government and Foreign Affairs. The government classes were pretty small, and I may have been the only female in most of them. I never felt the least bit ostracized or out of place. The professors were great." Many classmates indicated that they had excellent relationships with faculty members and counted some as mentors and friends. Barbara M. Golden Lynn (Arts and Sciences, '73) said, "I had close relationships with professors and President Shannon and still have friendships with some faculty at the University."

Ken Elzinga was and is an extremely popular economics professor who was named by several classmates as their "favorite professor." In communications for this book, he shared with me some surprises from the early days of coeducation:

> I am reminded of a time when I gave a talk to faculty in the College about how to teach Socratically and I was criticized by another faculty member (a woman in the Department of History) for this teaching method—because it was unfair to women. I was surprised (even astonished) by this criticism. I had thought one of the pedagogical strengths of my Antitrust Policy class was its Socratic teaching style. I was flabbergasted to be told that this was unfair to my female students. I asked some of the women in my class and they were flabbergasted to learn that a faculty member thought they could not handle Socratic teaching. I suppose if I were to point this out to my critic, she would have replied that my students were being deferential to my position of authority or were victimized by some kind of false consciousness.

When women arrived in 1970, there were virtually no female professors or faculty members, apart from some adjuncts who mainly taught foreign languages and graduate assistants who were TAs. While there were women faculty in the Schools of Education and Nursing, most of us would not encounter them until our third year, if ever. Several classmates indicated that, upon reflection, because the lack of female professors also meant a lack of female mentoring, and perhaps friendship, this is a part of a college experience that they wished they had had.

On My Honor as a Virginia Gentleman

Most of my classes were held in Cabell Hall (now called Old Cabell Hall), and hanging on the wall in many of the classrooms was a poster with the "honor pledge." We wrote this pledge on the bottom of our assignments:

On my honor as a Virginia gentleman,
I have neither given nor received aid on this (paper, exam, assignment).
Signature

When I first saw this posted, I remember wondering why someone hadn't changed the language before we came. By graduation, I came to believe that keeping the language was, in fact, intentional. By that time, we had stopped adhering to the provided wording and had made our own substitutions, typically writing "Virginia student" instead of "Virginia gentleman." It can be argued that "Virginia gentleman" and "Virginia student" are not synonymous, and the original language is explicitly evocative of the tradition and expectation of honor, which were then thought to be exemplified by males among the UVA community. And that would be one way to view this. Today, the language has been changed to "On my honor, I pledge that I have neither given nor received help on this assignment."

There is also the argument that in 1970, consideration of the use of gendered language and the impact it had was almost nonexistent. President Shannon's welcome letter in our orientation materials said the "gates to the Grounds of the University bears the inscription, 'Enter by this gateway and seek the way of honor, the light of truth, the will to work for men.'" Some women would report walking around these gates.

Another letter in our orientation materials came from H. S. Dabney, who was president of the National Bank and Trust Company in Charlottesville. In it, he welcomed us and encouraged us to open a checking account at the bank, which had a "banking office" in Newcomb Hall. He wrote, "During the past 150-year history of the University hundreds of thousands of men have preceeded [sic] you and have contributed tremendously to the enrichment, both of the University and this city. Thus, we genuinely look forward each fall to the arrival of the student body as a revitalizing element in our life here."[9]

Barracks Road Shopping Center added an insert from the *Daily Progress*, Charlottesville's hometown newspaper, to our orientation materials allowing merchants to advertise to new students. The cover illustration, depicting men through the ages until the final picture showed a man and a woman, read, "You've come a long way boys and so has Barracks

88 HERE TO STAY

The Charlottesville newspaper the *Daily Progress* gets into the act. (*Daily Progress*, September 30, 1970; author's collection)

Road Shopping Center." A women's clothing store, La Vogue, advertised directly to the new women students: "Mind Ever Matter? Sure that sharp little brain of yours got you to U. Va. in the first place, but how can a guy show off his date's mind! That's why smart girls make it a point to look great too."[10]

Dorm Life

Most women I surveyed indicated that dorm life worked for them—after some adjustments. The majority of us had corresponded by letters with our future roommate to discuss important decisions—for example, who would bring the eight-track tape system and who would bring the coffee pot. The spartan rooms would become our blank palettes. Some of us hung colorful blankets and posters, and my roommate and I purchased matching comforters and rugs, requiring a trip to Barracks Road

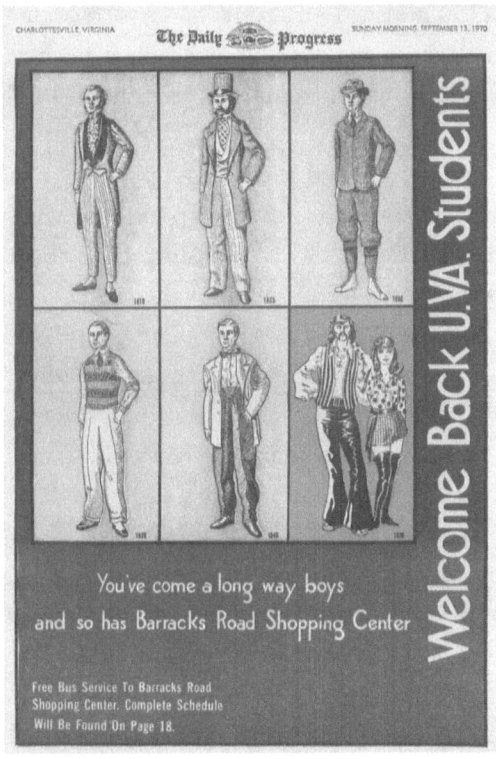

The *Daily Progress* documented the shift in student population in an advertising circular. (*Daily Progress*, September 13, 1970; author's collection)

Shopping Center. I remember spending most of my time after classes in my room, studying, listening to music, and napping, a habit many of us acquired during our college years.

One classmate noted, "I realized right away that my roommate came from a family with a lot more money than mine had when I saw she had shoes to match each outfit." Another classmate, who also recognized a wide gap between her family's resources and many of her suitemates said, "The money issue resolved itself when we quickly traded in our dresses and skirts for jeans and sweaters. That put us on a level playing field."

A few women reported making official room changes, working with the Housing Office to find a better fit. Most changes, within suites, were informally done, swapping roommates so that night owls roomed with night owls and early risers roomed with early risers. Even when roommates weren't entirely compatible, it usually worked out. After the first several weeks, most of us had established a routine, of sorts, trudging back to Alderman Library to study in the evening or heading down to Tuttle, another Alderman Road dorm, where there was a study lounge and a TV room for breaks.

The suite did not include a television, and with no cell phones, computers, or electronics to distract us, we would entertain ourselves. Many a study break was spent on the vinyl couches in deep conversations about things we were learning and things we were thinking. The single suite phone would ring from time to time—sometimes on the other end was a man asking someone out on a date, sometimes it was another woman friend. My roommate got calls, often late at night, about bridge games starting up at nearby dorms, and more often than not she would change out of her loungewear and into jeans and trek off. She usually wouldn't return until early morning.

Music was also a big part of dorm living with tape decks and record players occupying a corner of many rooms. Patricia (Pat) Gritis Lessard (Arts and Sciences, '74) recalls, "One of the sweetest memories of the first month was that on a great many nights—and I think it was at 11 p.m.—someone from the boys' dorms up the hill played 'Nights in White Satin' from the album *Days of Future Past* by the Moody Blues. I never knew who played it at full volume for all of us. I loved it then. I love it still. It always reminds me of the days when I was eighteen years old." Another classmate mentions the same memory of the nightly Moody Blues song but claims it was her female roommate who played it.

Karen Wester Marcus (Education, '71; M.Ed., '72) was the head counselor in Webb, a dorm that housed all women. It was Karen's responsibility to enforce the parietal hours, knocking on doors and, in her words, "kicking the guys out." She said some of her male counselor friends would come with her to escort the men out, worrying that Karen, about five feet tall with shoes on, might have some trouble. She said that she never needed their help, although she welcomed the support. In some cases, hours weren't enforced at all, and women shared their rooms with men all week long. One classmate recalls once returning to her room to find that her roommate and her roommate's boyfriend had confiscated her bed and were enjoying a now "double bed." She later moved in with a friend whose roommate left during orientation. While housing never officially approved the move, she stayed in the new room throughout her first year.

One classmate wrote in the 1998 survey, "1st year suites were HORRIBLE for privacy!" She continued, "Let me be blunt: If I hadn't met my husband during my 1st year, I never would have stayed at U.Va. My memories of the University are of dorm parties (I was a non-drinker), aloof and uninteresting professors, and rampant drug use and promiscuity. Since I had nothing to do with the latter, I mostly tried to shelter myself from many activities."

Clothes Make the Man—and Woman

For well over a century, it is reported that students at UVA wore coats and ties to their classes. And while the arrival of women has often been blamed for the demise of that formal tradition, history indicates that the coat and tie was on its way out years before our cadre of undergraduate women arrived in 1970. During the 1960s, men began to dress more casually, and jeans and T-shirts were as common as khakis and sports coats. Prior to being named chair of the committee to investigate coeducation, T. Braxton Woody lamented, "It was distressing to see great traditions passing away: 'The tradition of gentlemanly dress is slowly dying.'"[11]

Alarie Tennille (Arts and Sciences, '74) remembers, "My brother told me that I would need to wear dresses to class since the men wore ties. The summer before I left for college, my best friend made me a bunch of dresses. I thought I was ready. When I got to UVA, I realized that most of the girls had no intention of wearing dresses. They wore jeans and sometimes skirts, but never the kind of dresses I brought. I didn't have money for new clothes, so I wore what I brought, and I survived."

UVA alumna Katie Couric (Arts and Sciences, '79) writes in her memoir, *Going There*, about being "curious about the sorority scene" and realizing at the first meeting that her clothing was not right. She quickly bought "headbands, khakis, and Fair Isle sweaters" and became, in her words, "Katie 2.0."[12]

My friends and I sported bellbottoms, army shirts, and retro clothing from Salvation Army. Some students still dressed up for football games and the parties before and after, especially men in fraternities and their dates. And there were women who still wore dresses and skirts and men who often wore a sport coat and tie with their jeans. But there was no question that casual dress had become the default.

Virginius Dabney, the Pulitzer Prize–winning writer, son of a faculty member, and direct descendant of Jefferson through his mother, chronicled UVA history in several volumes. He writes that the women, specifically our class of women, brought a new "low" standard of dress to the university:

> The hundreds of girls who entered in 1970 seemed to want to outdo the boys in the slovenliness of their dress. As was the prevailing custom during that period throughout the United States, both groups garbed themselves in patched, faded, frayed blue jeans. The boys wore long, unkempt hair and beat-up shoes. Both groups began dressing more neatly as the years passed, but in 1970 the emphasis was on the sloppiest conceivable attire.[13]

Although I don't recall the "slovenliness" of our dress or an attempt to "outdo the boys," the writings of Dabney make one thing crystal clear—there were those who believed then, and probably always will, that the decline of dress at the university, if not caused by coeducation, was certainly correlated with it.

Party School

Many of us had heard that there were rankings and ratings of colleges based on student "partying." The word on Grounds was that *Playboy* magazine had rated UVA as one of the top party schools in the country and that, in the early 1970s, Easters Weekend, held the week after Easter, was rated by the magazine as "the best party in America."[14] Big weekends like Homecomings and Easters were celebrated with big parties. There were often live bands, sometimes mud pits, and always plenty of alcohol. It should be noted that "Easters" got so raucous, and the drinking so excessive, that it was officially banned in 1982.

Whether true or not, it was said that after naming some other well-known "party" schools in a late 1960s *Playboy* article, UVA had the distinct "honor" of being set apart from the others by an asterisk and the comment "The University of Virginia isn't rated because it would be unfair to rank professionals with amateurs." This is likely an urban myth, and other schools believe they were the ones set apart as the professional. What *Playboy* has acknowledged is that there was the ability to alter content regionally, and so what UVA alumni remember could in fact be true. In any event, alcohol was a standard at most parties, even in the dorms. And on special occasions or at mixers, hard liquor was the norm.

One classmate said, "I remember learning that Singapore Slings were very potent and have never had another one." For the uninformed, a Singapore Sling is a cocktail made from gin, liqueurs, and fruit juice. Another student said that thanks to her college experiences, she still can't stand the smell of bourbon. Smoking pot was also part of the party scene, but it more often was done in area fields or off-Grounds' apartments where there seemed to be less risk of an arrest.

Fraternity parties were a whole different animal. Fraternity members visited us in the dorms during Rush with invitations to "participate." When we asked what that meant exactly, the answers were evasive. Invitations also came by mail to parties and mixers, which some of us would attend, but it was clear fairly quickly that fraternities had no real intention of making us members. Little sisters? Sure. Social members? Possibly. But few of us were interested. During our tenure women would often be linked to a certain fraternity through male friends or a boyfriend.

Homecomings was our first big weekend of the school year. Some women had experienced a UVA party weekend while in high school, visiting a boyfriend or male friend, but many of us were new to the festivities. A Friday mixer or "smoker," with alcohol, Saturday football game, with alcohol, Saturday evening concert, with alcohol, followed by a party at the fraternity house with a band—and lots of alcohol. As previously mentioned, few of us had dates for the first big weekend. Many of our male classmates had made plans—sometimes months in advance—to bring a date from a neighboring college, typically, and traditionally an "all-girls' school."

Imports Go Home

Through no fault of their own, we began referring to women who came to events at UVA from other schools as "imports." And that Homecomings weekend, as we stood on our balconies on a beautiful fall Friday afternoon, watching well-dressed, well-groomed women from Virginia's "women's schools" arrive, something didn't sit well with us. The women, all wearing dresses, were accompanied by a male UVA student, often in coat and tie, who carried their suitcase into a dorm. The guys had convinced their women friends from high school, their sisters, or their lab partners to let their dates stay with them. One classmate recalls "Boos" coming from the balconies as women arrived, and another recalls a large banner with "Imports Go Home" written on it hanging from the railing outside a neighboring suite. This all feels shameful looking back.

Dick Lynch (Arts and Sciences, '71), a fourth-year student in 1970, lived his first semester of that year in an Alderman Road dorm. He was a "friend of the suite," in this case my suite in Maupin, a term perhaps coined by one of our classmates. Lynch recalls a message posted over the community mailboxes in Tuttle Dormitory that said something to the effect of, "Hey Guys! Why don't you ask a UVA woman to Homecomings? You won't even have to pay for a ticket to the football game!"

Laura Funkhouser (Arts and Sciences, '74), in an October 26, 1970, article in the *Cavalier Daily* entitled "Va. Gentlewomen Meet a Man's World," states as the sentiment of "many of the first-year women, 'Although the University is now coeducational in name, it may take time for it to be coeducational in spirit.'" The article explores transition issues facing the new women, "who are having to brave the one-to-twenty ratio both in the crowded classrooms of Cabell Hall and in their dorm rooms on somewhat lonely weekends." Laura quotes one woman as saying, "There is a definite lack of social life for us." Another states, "The upperclassmen steer clear of us because they think we have it made."[15]

Finding Our People

Some women who responded to my survey indicated that the partying, while exciting at first, got old. One classmate said that she went to mixers and frat parties the first few months but found out quickly that you really couldn't meet people that way. Her assessment was that most parties were loud and full of drunken, horny guys.

There were other ways to socialize, and we found them—movies at Wilson Hall, political forums and discussions, dance groups. One classmate says her negative memories were largely confined to those first days. "Everything got better after that," she said. Most of us hung out with our suitemates, and some of us paired up with boyfriends quickly. Barbara Willette (Arts and Sciences, '74) remembers, "It was much easier to make friends than in high school. The cliques and hierarchies were mostly gone. People who wouldn't have said boo to me in high school were friendly at college because we were all new there."

Others connected with students in their classes, male and female, and studied together or took trips to Skyline Drive or Monticello. Elizabeth Gress Muenster Hunt (Arts and Sciences, '74) said, "I think our class 'toned down' the bawdy fraternity scene, and generally made the college a little quieter and more serious."

Some women in the class had older brothers at UVA, and if they had a car, and many did, we would get them and a friend to take us and a few suitemates to dinner—everyone paying their own way, of course—or to the mountains, or exploring Charlottesville. Many first-year students had friends, both male and female, from high school attending the university and, when yearning for the familiar, would eat dinner or study with old friends. Some first-years went home most or many weekends. There was always a way to hitch a ride with a fellow student to northern Virginia or Richmond or Norfolk. Some women had boyfriends from high school who were still in their hometown or at a different college, and the women would travel many weekends to see them. We were still figuring out what to do with these unstructured, unsupervised blocks of time. Studying was always an option, and for some, Alderman Library was actually a place to meet people, too.

And, of course, there were those of us who were lonely. And homesick. And unsure how to find our footing. Some of us were accustomed to more privacy than dorm life afforded, and the constant noise and other people around were wearing. One classmate recalls sitting at Newcomb Hall with a suitemate, mid-conversation, when a male student sat down at their table. "It was always like this," she said. "The men somehow thought we would want them there. That our conversations weren't important. We found this very aggravating." Another said she was eating by herself when a male student sat down and the first thing out of his mouth was "Are you on birth control?" When she didn't respond, he continued, "You should be."

Annette Gibbs, in 1991, talked about the environment we found on our arrival.

> There were a lot of fraternities, but no women's sororities, no social sororities at all; much less service fraternities or sororities, which later came when we got larger numbers of Black students, both men and women. But there were no honorary groups for women. One of the biggest problems [was] that there were no athletic facilities, there were no intramurals, there were no club sports for women. And, of course, every time we tried to get women to go to the gym, the guys ran them out.[16]

In the conclusions Louise Robertson draws from the twenty-eight surveys she conducted in 1985 with women from our class, she reported that women expressed being "oddities" and how difficult that was.[17] More than half of the respondents reported significant transition issues. Phyllis Leffler writes that women were "consciously marginalized by male students and by university administrators."[18] During a 2021 webinar called "Our Evolving Narrative: Alumnae Reflections across Generations," which was a follow-up to the Alumni Association's virtual summit, ReTold, Mary Ann Huey (Arts and Sciences, '75) said she and others sometimes felt like "ornaments."[19]

The Tradition of Rolling

Dennis Phelan (Arts and Sciences, '74), who came to UVA from Chicago, said he really didn't understand the anti-female sentiment expressed by some of his fellow male classmates. His roommate and friends on the hall were happy to have women at UVA. They did, however, all try the dating tradition known as "rolling." He described a typical rolling experience as "finding someone with a car, piling in, and drinking all the way to a girls' school. We'd find a girls' dorm, and we would talk to the housemother in the lobby. She would call upstairs and see if any girls wanted to go out with us UVA men, and we would spend the evening with these 'dates,' before rolling back to Charlottesville. On the return trip, we would often stop in Crozet at Ida's Diner. It was a hole-in-the-wall spot on Route 250 West. Hamburgers cost 25 cents—it was heaven."

My husband, Larry, said this about rolling: "Usually it was one guy who had a girlfriend, a friend from high school, or some connection to the women's school, and they would call up someone there and arrange for the group of guys to drive out and have dates. We might go to a concert or a party or something like that there. But it was not a good situation, because we didn't know the women, so it was awkward when we'd get there. Once the women came to UVA in 1970, it was much more fun to bump into folks in the cafeteria and walking to and from class. It was just more normal, a more natural environment."

Barry Parkhill (Education, '73), agreed with his friend and teammate's assessment. "The rolling was really more about male bonding and less about the dates. And, every year there were [car] accidents so it wasn't a good thing."

More than one female classmate commented that men at UVA, particularly those in fraternities, were accustomed to dating a woman on a weekend and then not feeling any responsibility after dropping her off. Perhaps that behavior was a byproduct of rolling, a custom that often resulted in a date being random, or the friend of another man's girlfriend. Rolling would continue beyond our tenure at UVA, but to a lesser extent. The practice of drinking and driving resulted in tragedies, both at UVA and elsewhere. Anecdotally, the increase in education and awareness around driving under the influence means most young people today are much more responsible than we were when it comes to making such decisions.

Safety

While most of us felt safe in our dorms, unlocked suite doors led to several scary encounters. On at least one occasion, and likely more, an unknown man wandered into the group bathroom, frightening a woman who was in the shower. A number of classmates recount having had "close calls," and there were also some assaults. Safety was something we all had to pay attention to throughout our four years in Charlottesville. I would discover that making UVA safer was a long-fought battle that began years before we set foot on Grounds in 1970.

It would be many years before UVA and other colleges and universities would be pressured into reporting the numbers of crimes, from thefts to assaults and rapes, that occurred on their campuses. Parents of female students, specifically, were often dismayed to learn the number of physical and sexual assaults at the colleges their daughters would attend. Part of any parent's calculus in the important decision of where their daughter would spend her first years living independently was how safe she would be.

Regarding safety for women, in Mary Whitney's last report to the UVA administration, discussed in chapter 2, she intentionally, I suspect, begins her twelve-page missive with her concerns about women's safety.[20] Gibbs, who joined the administration the day after Whitney left, spoke to the same issue in a 1991 oral history interview:

> I think one of the most difficult things of implementing coeducation, in addition to the things I mentioned, was the fact that the Grounds were very, very dark then. It just was not a safe and secure place to be because the University of Virginia had received considerable publicity about its coeducation and implementing coeducation, the year after Princeton. And in many ways, I used the Princeton model of coeducation here. But, here we were fighting a myth about how the Grounds should be reasonably dark at night because of the shadows of Mr. Jefferson, and so forth. And we didn't want to interrupt the architectural beauty of the Lawn and the traditional aspects. But it just was not a safe place.

She continued, "So, over several months, and in fact a year and a half, we began to attack the problem of darkness, if you will, by using different kinds of illumination, focused in different [directions], at different times of night to not create glares but in keeping with the architectural beauty of the Lawn and the ranges and even near the buildings."[21]

I, as much as anybody, love the beauty of UVA's Grounds. But it is disconcerting, to say the least, that when weighing measures to keep members of the student body safe from harm, the aesthetics of the Grounds took precedence.

Rhythms and Routines

The chaos and craziness of the first month eventually died down, and most of us settled into our own schedule of attending classes, studying, and socializing. We made friends, we dated, we hung out with our roommate and suitemates. In most suites, there was a group of guys who became what we called "friends of the suite." In coed dorms, they were often the male students who lived in the same dorm. These friends usually didn't date anyone in the suite, but more often they sat with a group of us in the large living area and just hung out, or in the vernacular of the day, "shot the bull." One of our "suite friends" had a motorcycle and would take each of us for rides, often stopping at some place for food to break the mealtime monotony of on-Grounds dining, such as Newcomb Hall and the Glass Hat. Scott McWalter (Arts and Sciences, '74) remembers, "My buddies and I connected with a suite in Webb, and we found women who were fun to be around and enjoyed many of the things we did. It was a real plus to have these women as friends."

The men who began as first-year students with us in 1970 knew that they were part of the class that included the first group of undergraduate women, but to some, it was insignificant. Robert (Bob) McKeag (Education, '75) arrived from Erie, Pennsylvania, on a basketball scholarship. He recalls, "Not knowing much about the traditional male culture at UVA, it seemed very normal to me to have the first-year women in our classes and around the Grounds."

Karen Wester Marcus said that she connected with guys from her high school when she transferred from Mary Washington, and many were in the same fraternity. They invited her and the first-year women she advised to their parties and to come over and hang out. By the second semester of her final year at UVA, she paid to eat dinner at the frat house and spent much of her time there. There were other women, too, who would find a group of mostly men with whom they would spend their down time.

Finding Our Own Path

To this day, it still seems amazing that coeducation happened at UVA without much fanfare from the administration or the media. The *Cavalier Daily* reported on our entry the first week, and there were occasional articles after that, but it was low-key by most standards. I don't recall nor could I find any mention of the fact that our entry corresponded with the fiftieth anniversary of a woman's right to vote. One classmate recalls an event during orientation recognizing the historical significance of our enrollment, something I don't remember and haven't been able to confirm from orientation materials or the official schedule. Granted, social media wasn't part of our world then, but by all accounts, we were mostly left to figure things out on our own. Few recall much interaction with advisors or counselors, although there were noted exceptions. The seventeen female Echols scholars had a law school faculty member, Charles Whitebread, living in their dorm, and some that I interviewed reported that he provided support and assistance.

Gibbs said this approach was intentional and attributed it to Shannon's desire to treat everyone equally. He believed, she said, that just like the male students, women should and would let it be known what they needed and wanted. The logic of that, given the power dynamics at play, isn't simple. In some cases, this plan seemed to have worked. However, the next chapter discusses at least one area where the "let things evolve" philosophy put women at risk and reverberated for years after we were gone.

FIVE

... TO STAY

> It actually doesn't take much to be considered a difficult woman. That's why there are so many of us.
> —Jane Goodall

IN THE FALL OF 1971, we were joined by approximately 550 more women.[1] Unlike for our class, though, I was unable to locate the form Dean Ern would have completed for the State Council of Higher Education for Virginia (SCHEV) with that exact information. The number of applications for admittance into the second class of women, however, were reportedly threefold what they had been when we applied, and even with the additional slots, gaining admittance in 1971 was more difficult than it had been in 1970. The Office of Institutional Research and Analytics at the University of Virginia reported that average SAT scores for matriculants in 1971 increased for both verbal and math.[2]

The vocal minority of students and faculty who clung to the Jeffersonian tradition of an all-male university and who were steadfastly against coeducation became less visible and less vocal over the next few years. Some graduated, some were co-opted by the reality of a thriving coeducational university, and some probably lost interest in the issue. Looking back in 2024, the resistance to coeducation in the late 1960s seems hard to believe.

Tom Bagby (Arts and Sciences, '72), was the chair of the Honor Committee in 1971–72. He was a strong supporter of coeducation. Involved in just about every aspect of academic and student life, he recently acknowledged that even during the second year of coeducation, there were still men who wanted things to return to pre-coeducation days. Those who wore the BBTOU (Bring Back the Old U) buttons, though, were a dying breed. "Most of those who were doubtful it would work were soon won over," Tom said. "When sitting in a class with women students, it quickly became evident to everyone that they were smart and prepared and that they belonged."

Another man I interviewed said female classmates were creative and had interesting things to say. As a group, we were excelling academically, choosing majors, and some were beginning the process of transferring into one of the other schools (e.g., commerce, architecture, or education).

Many nursing students faced different challenges, and some report struggling academically, in part because they were encountering undergraduate classes that were designed for pre-med students. Some women reported that they were welcomed into the mostly male classes made up of pre-med students because the men believed that the women would make up the bottom of the grading curve. Other women indicated that the nursing students who transferred to UVA from other schools for their third year benefited from the programs at their previous schools that were specifically designed to prepare them for a nursing degree.

For the transfer students, their GPAs started anew at UVA, while those who had attended UVA in their first and second years had cumulative GPAs. "We bitterly complained but nothing was done," noted Susanna Chiocca Mannix (Nursing, '74). "However, the next few years UVA did establish a strong pre-nursing program."

Baby Steps

Annette Gibbs, in a 1991 oral history interview, speaks to the changes that were made for our second year and the process of making that happen:

> Mr. Shannon asked me what the two main imperative needs for coeducation were, after we got past the physical kinds of things. It didn't take me long to decide. I thought that a women's sports director or a person to work

with women's athletics was just an absolute must, and the corresponding facilities and schedules for that. And I remember that we did hire someone, Barbara Kelly. And we finally worked out a program whereby women for a large part of the day and many evenings could have Memorial Gym. And within, I would say, three semesters, this university had a women's athletic or sports program that grew into the national stature that it is now—that can compete with anybody. But it was difficult to get women's athletics, club sports and so forth going.

Gibbs continued:

> The second problem we had is that there was no safe place for women to go for recreation or a cup of coffee or a glass of wine or whatever. The men had not only their fraternities, but they had "The Corner" there; the notorious corner across from the old hospital. But women did not feel safe going to those places alone at night—the Grounds were still dark. And we began to think of ways to renovate Newcomb Hall. Then it was called The Rathskeller, years ago. And, of course, that facility has gone through several updatings, if you will, in terms of students' needs and desires. But it was just bad that women didn't have a safe place to go, to hang out, if you will, like the fraternities.[3]

Unintended Consequences of Transition Plan

"After the first year, the additional students created a crisis in student housing," Jan Gaylord Owen writes in her Columbia University doctoral dissertation about the Shannon years. "As planned growth began to be realized, housing became even more [of] a major concern for students than for the administrators. In addition to the special housing needs that accompanied the presence of undergraduate women, more and more students of both sexes found themselves competing for fewer and fewer available spaces. They would increasingly have to find housing on the open market within the community of Charlottesville. Off-campus housing, which had once been a privilege reserved for upperclassmen, now became a growing necessity."[4]

I, like many of my classmates, made the move off campus my second year at UVA. Late in the spring of 1971, a male friend who was graduating stopped by my suite with exciting news. He said friends of his who had been renting a small house across from the medical school were all leaving and would recommend us to their landlord. He drove me to look at the house, 300 Park Place, which was affordable and well designed for at least four people, and best of all, it was within walking distance to the Grounds and the Corner. (In an actual case of "paving paradise to put up a parking lot," to paraphrase Joni Mitchell's "Big Yellow Taxi," the house is no longer there, nor the surrounding neighborhood or street. It was razed and incorporated into the Virginia Medical Center complex years ago.) I immediately checked with three friends who were also looking for housing, and they too were excited about the prospect of living in a house rather than an apartment. We quickly signed a lease, and two of these women and I were housemates the remaining three years and are still the dearest of friends today.

There were simply more students than there were places to live on Grounds. Many women and men who expected to live in university dorms their second year were forced to look elsewhere. There had been plans to build another dorm for upper-class women, but that didn't materialize, and almost all the dorm space was needed for the expanding first-year population. Some administrators attributed the flight of students to apartments and houses surrounding the Grounds as a backlash to the suite-style living accommodations.[5] The large communal room with five shared bedrooms and one large bathroom with a single shower didn't feel "homey" or cozy. At least a few of my classmates did not consider the suite setup to be ideal, but the reality was that for every student who preferred off-Grounds housing, there were just as many who would have liked to stay in the dorms another year. Fraternities offered rooms in the fraternity houses to their members. In fact, in some cases, second-year students were required to live there. Initially there was only one social sorority, Zeta Tau Alpha, and it originally only rushed and pledged nursing students. Alison Ingram (Engineering, '75) describes joining, along with a small cohort of non-nursing students, her first year and living in the house her second year. The sorority dissolved the end of that year and later reorganized with new membership. By our third year there would be several sororities for Black women, and more followed with primarily white members after we graduated.

Many first-year women applied to be counselors in the dorms for their second year, renamed resident advisors, or RAs, not only because the position appealed to them, but also because they would save money on their living expenses, and this would solve their housing problem.[6]

Involved in Everything

By our second, third, and fourth years, we were involved in organizations and student government and becoming more deeply entrenched in the fabric of the UVA community. We were helping organize new clubs, such as the Riding Club and the French Club, and expanding existing clubs and organizations. The numbers of women who would volunteer, tutor, and become "Big Sisters" through the Madison House program increased the size of their program substantially. In *Mr. Jefferson's University*, Virginius Dabney would write that one unpredicted and positive consequence of coeducation was a new spirit of service.[7]

Some of the Black women in our class reported involvement with the Black Student Alliance (BSA), which was started at UVA in 1969 as the Black Students for Freedom and was renamed in 1971.[8] BSA not only

Many women found their way to Madison House and their programs working with area children. (1974 *Corks and Curls*)

Black Student Alliance members provided assistance to children in the Charlottesville community. (1974 *Corks and Curls*)

functioned to identify and pursue improvements in areas of unequal and discriminatory practices; it was also the main social support for Black students at UVA. Although the numbers of Black students increased substantially in 1970, they were still a small fraction of the total number of students at the university. In 1970, four Black scholarship student athletes—Kent Merritt, Harrison Davis, Stanley Land, and John Rainey—integrated UVA's football team, and Al Drummond became the first Black scholarship student athlete to join UVA's men's basketball team. Although more Black students would receive football scholarships in the subsequent years, Al would remain the only Black basketball player on a scholarship during his four-year tenure at the university.

One holdout when it came to admitting women was the Jefferson Literary and Debating Society, known as the Jefferson Society, which still had bylaws requiring members to be male. In 1971, a female student threatened to sue the society, but before that happened, the bylaws were changed in a strategic move by the vice president.[9] Chapter 6 includes a profile of the Jefferson Society's first female member, Barbara M. Golden

In 1972, for the first time, first-year women were admitted in the same pool with men instead of in addition to them. (*Cavalier Daily*, September 12, 1972)

Coed Threatens Law Suit Against Jefferson Society

By RICHARD PETTY and BILL PATTERSON

The Jefferson Literary and Debating Society has been threatened with a lawsuit if it fails to vote for the admission of women to the society at its regular meeting tomorrow.

Barbara K. Sugarman, a fourth-year student in the School of Education, told The Cavalier Daily, "I will bring a lawsuit immediately if the vote is not favorable." Mrs. Sugarman was interviewed by the society last semester but was denied membership.

"At the time I felt I was given a fair interview and thought I might be accepted," Mrs. Sugarman said. "When I was not accepted solely on the basis of my sex I was going to sue the society then, but I was convinced to let Student Council handle it."

"I think the society is being very close-minded," Mrs. Sugarman stated. "They are relegating women to the position that Blacks held at the University ten years ago."

Divided Issue

Members of the society are divided on the issue of coeducation. Mike Lynn, a current member, is a strong advocate for the admission of women.

Mr. Lynn stated that "besides the familiar issues of equality and giving women the same opportunities at the University that the men have, there is another issue which is more practical."

"There is the important question of the survival of the Jefferson Society in the future," he continued. "The society needs to take in the best possible members, and they are often women."

Gentleman's Club

Alex Simon, a third year student and current member of the Hall, is strongly opposed to the movement to coeducate the Jefferson Society. "The Hall has a dual function to serve as a debating society and a gentleman's club," Mr. Simon said.

"The introduction of women," he continued, "would completely alter the atmosphere of the hall. The introduction of women would cause the male members to try to pick up the female members of the Hall."

"As the University expands," Mr. Simon stated, "women will have more than adequate educational opportunities without membership in the Hall."

"Coeducation is not necessary for the survival of the Hall," he said. "The Hall has better leadership in office this semester than it has had in several years. The Hall is performing its dual function."

Photo By Charley Sands
Barbara Sugarman
Threatens To Sue Jefferson Society

Officers, Sex Bias

for not advising non-administrative members of the committee of President Edgar F. Shannon's announced cutback in next year's entering class before the meeting. "It was so obvious that administrative members of the committee were well-informed beforehand," he said.

Challenging the holdouts. (*Cavalier Daily*, February 10, 1972)

Lynn (Arts and Sciences, '73), who was admitted in 1972, and describes the strategy employed by her then boyfriend, now husband, to make that happen.

Women's and Men's Athletics

In 1971, Barbara Kelly was hired as director of intramurals and physical education, the first female physical education staff member.[10] She worked diligently to strengthen club sports and find locker rooms, gym space, and fields where women could practice and play. As an aside, in the years prior to women's sports teams becoming intercollegiate, if there were not enough women to create an intramural or club sports team, it was common for women who weren't full-time students, or who were affiliated with the university in a different capacity, to participate. During the 1973–74 academic year, UVA fielded its first intercollegiate women's teams in basketball, field hockey, and tennis.

Around this time, the men's basketball program was taking off. Early in the second semester of our first year, for the first time in many years, the men's basketball team was ranked in the top twenty nationally. This resulted in a huge increase in student interest in attending home

The author, *top left*, with a group of her Maupin dormmates en route to the National Invitation Tournament at Madison Square Garden in 1971. (Author's collection)

Field hockey was one of the first intercollegiate sports offered at UVA for women. (1974 *Corks and Curls*)

basketball games at the now razed University Hall (U-Hall), lovingly called the Clamshell for its unique round structure and scalloped roof. Previously, any student could walk into a game and have a seat, with plenty of empty seats for coats and bags. But after the somewhat surprising ranking, tickets became a hot commodity. To nab one, we began camping out in front of the ticket office the night before they were available to students, bringing sleeping bags, pillows, food, cards, and a party-like spirit. For many of us, this was a way to make new friends—a social event in and of itself.

Barry Parkhill (Education, '73) was a star player on UVA's basketball team from 1969 to 1973 and played a major role in the team receiving the national ranking, as well as having winning seasons during our tenure at UVA. I asked him in 2022 whether he thought the sellout games during that time and the student experience of "camping out" at U-Hall for seats would have happened without women students. "That's hard to answer," Parkhill said from his office at the university, where he is currently associate athletic director. "All I know is that things were very different from the games my first year at the university when women weren't in attendance in any significant numbers. I only wish I had had the money to take pizzas to all the students spending the night at U-Hall. The crowds we had the remainder of my time at UVA made playing ball really great."

Coed water polo was a big hit. (1974 *Corks and Curls*)

For some of us who didn't play sports, being able to watch a polo match on a beautiful spring day or sit on the hill in Scott Stadium for a football game when the leaves on the trees ringing the field were golden and russet and crimson are memories that we cherish. To this day, I can see in my mind's eye the long-gone baseball stadium at Lambeth Field, sans the dorms that are there today, and the concrete steps placed into the hillside that for some inexplicable reason were quite comfortable. There was no better view of the mountains to the west and no better way to spend a sunny, spring afternoon.

The Greek Life

The first Greek letter fraternities began in America in the 1700s. Since then, the presence of these social and sometimes professional societies has grown on college campuses. At UVA in the early 1970s, fraternities equaled mixers, parties, and tailgating at football games. Even as non-members, women quickly became familiar with the different fraternities,

Even without sororities, women partook in Greek life. (1973 *Corks and Curls*)

as well as the reputation of their members. A couple of houses considered themselves, and were often thought of, as the "elites," their members being the upper echelon of the privileged. Several fraternities considered "southern" were greatly influenced by "Old U" traditions and culture; another had a strong tradition of Jewish membership. In the dean of students' files from our years, there are multiple memos about membership issues and whether fraternities were engaged in exclusionary practices related to race.[11] There are indications of Black members in fraternity rosters and memos; however, pictures in the UVA Yearbook, *Corks and Curls*, whose name has its own questionable past relative to race, would counter that claim. In 1973, chapters of historically Black fraternities and sororities were started at the University: Alpha Kappa Alpha, Omega Psi Phi, and Delta Sigma Theta.

Dean Ern and former president Casteen both indicated that some of the anti-coeducation sentiment, both initial and residual, came from fraternities. It seems that some fraternities, specifically those considered the most conservative and traditional, were more vocal. One classmate noted that UVA was a much more conservative school than she had realized when she decided to attend. That conservatism, some said, hampered the efforts for change. There appears to be some congruence with the anti-coeducation attitudes and the mythology associated with "the Virginia Gentleman."

In 2014, *Rolling Stone* magazine would call this fraternity ditty the "traditional University of Virginia fight song" (note: RMWC is Randolph Macon Women's College):[12]

> From Rugby Road to Vinegar Hill, we're gonna get drunk tonight
> The faculty's afraid of us, they know we're right
> So fill up your cups, your loving cups, as full as full can be
> As long as love and liquor last, we'll drink to the U of V.
>
> All you girls from Mary Washington
> And RMWC, never let a Cavalier an inch above your knee.
> He'll take you to his fraternity house and fill you full of beer.
> And soon you'll be the mother of a bastard Cavalier!

Rugby Road was home to most of the fraternities. The gorgeous brick mansions that housed the fraternities were imposing and striking, making the sometimes dilapidated and grungy interiors, smelling of stale beer, surprising. There is no question that a sizable portion of male students were interested in membership in a fraternity. Some would pledge but not join, others would pledge, join, and then quit as upperclassmen, when the cost of the yearly dues became a challenge. But most men who joined as first-year students would remain members their four years at college, often returning even after they graduated for big weekends or fraternity reunions. From year to year, the percentage of male students who were members of a fraternity changes. Some decades have seen surges in membership while others have seen diminished numbers. What has remained a constant, however, is that UVA's social life is inextricably tied to the Greek system, which made the female student body's initial disinterest in sororities all the more confusing.

Sororities or Not?

Following the court decision in October 1969, Mary Whitney sent a memo to D. Alan Williams, dean of student affairs, about the one sorority on Grounds, Alpha Zeta Tau, and their interest in rushing the women who would be entering in 1970. Previously considered a "nursing sorority," the membership reported at that time was very low. Whitney advised against allowing Alpha Zeta Tau to rush the incoming women because she stated that, in her experience, this sorority did not extend invitations to Black women, and her assumption was that there would be Black women entering with the class of 1974.[13]

When Annette Gibbs assumed the position of associate dean, taking on, in her words, "the coeducation transition," she reported being immediately contacted by national sorority organizations that expressed interest in opening chapters at UVA. She said she met with the women in our class, which Dickie McMullan (Arts and Sciences, '74) remembered as well. When Gibbs asked if there was any interest in joining a sorority, Dickie said, "The women in the room looked around at each other and said, 'This is our sorority.'" No one was terribly interested. Indeed, according to her dissertation, when E. A. Mayer, a doctoral student and assistant dean, interviewed female students at the beginning of second semester, forty-eight of the fifty interviewees answered the question "Do you have any interest in joining a sorority?" with "No."[14]

Gibbs, in a phone call, agreed with Dickie's assessment. She said she told the presidents of the national organizations, "Thanks, but no thanks." She said, "I had to tell them to fly their private planes home."

In her chapter titled "Women's Admission to the University of Virginia: Tradition Transformed," Elizabeth Ihle posits that the "kind of woman" accepted as students those first few years might have had a lot to do with the initial disinterest in sororities.[15] Sororities, historically, are more popular in the South, and 83 percent of the women in the first class were from Virginia, and some of the out-of-state women were from southern states as well. I'm uncertain whether Ihle is correct, but in any event, interest in sororities would shift as the number of women increased, and by our fourth year, sororities were sprouting up at UVA.

Two Steps Forward, One Step Back

As mentioned in the beginning of the chapter, the anti-coeducation sentiments among various factions were dissipating with time. But they were by no means gone entirely. My housemate, Annette Jorgensen McKeag (Education, '74), remembers taking the class "The History of the University," when the professor, a bow-tied elderly man, stated with no hesitation or concern for the women students in attendance that the university was ruined when women were admitted.

Karen Brainard (Nursing, '74), interested in becoming a doctor, made an appointment to see the dean of UVA's Medical School. She expressed her interest in possibly attending UVA's Medical School after graduating with her degree in nursing. He told her they would not consider any of her undergraduate credits in nursing because they did not deem those courses to be college-level credits.

Joan Kennedy (Architecture, '74), interested in a degree in architecture, was told women were not architects. It was suggested that perhaps she might be interested in being a city planner.

Sometimes when you're in the middle of a shift, it's hard to know how substantial the change is. With each passing year any doubts we might have had about belonging at UVA lessened. Although we weren't successful in every endeavor, we were meeting with enough success to know that predictions that we would struggle with the coursework were unfounded. Most of us had just as many male friends as female friends, and as more men who never knew anything but a UVA with women students took their place among us, the university recalibrated.

Carolyn Hurlburt (Arts and Sciences, '74), who is now a retired professional actor, reflected on the fact she never faced any discrimination at UVA. "I believe that is because I was a drama major and involved in plays throughout my years at the University," she said. "There were older students and others involved that really never thought like that."

By 1980, just ten years after we arrived, undergraduate women outnumbered men at UVA. Larry Sabato (Arts and Sciences, '74) astutely observed, "It actually says something about how quickly institutions can be transformed."

The theater department's production of *Godspell*. (1974 *Corks and Curls*)

Susan Tyler Hitchcock (GSAS, '78) arrived in Charlottesville in 1975 to pursue her Ph.D. in English. She shared an office with former President Shannon but says she didn't know at the time what had recently transpired at UVA. It wasn't until later that she learned about the history that had been made, and her office mate's key role in it, the previous five years.

Mavis Hetherington, at ninety-five years old, recalled her first years at UVA. Hired as one of the first tenured female professors, Hetherington was a veteran of breaking glass ceilings. She was the first female psychology professor at University of Wisconsin, where she worked before accepting a position at UVA. She laughed when she talked about the concerns voiced about female students' ability to do the work. "The women were at the top of the class in every course I taught," she said. "It was nonsense to think they weren't as smart or capable as men."

The Only Way Out Is Through

For many, the amount of classwork was intense and unexpected. The outside reading and writing assignments were challenging, and there was the added pressure to do well, to prove ourselves. Some of us realized our initial thoughts about majors and careers beyond college were not what we really wanted. As much as we wanted to stay "footloose and fancy-free," the real world loomed large.

By the time we were in our fourth year, we had found "our people" and were filling our class schedule and free time with whatever we determined was most important and interesting. Some of us coupled up with boyfriends, who turned into fiancés, who turned into husbands. Fifty years later, some of us, me included, are still married to our UVA boyfriends.

Many of us worked part-time jobs, on Grounds or off, to help pay for expenses, clothes, food, and travel. Some of us spent time with professionals who worked in the fields we were studying, although the formal "internships" of today were unheard of. We began to consider life after UVA, complete with entry-level jobs, and many of us began making treks to the Career Center and meeting with the few counselors there who helped with job searches. Lots of us, encouraged by professors and administrators, applied to graduate school and professional schools, often at UVA.

As time went on, we declared majors in the College of Arts and Sciences, and some of us transferred to the School of Nursing and the School of Education, a few to the School of Architecture, and a few to the School of Commerce. Slots for the School of Education and School of Nursing were very competitive, with additional students, sometimes with better grades, transferring into the programs from nearby schools. Carolyn Joyner Smith (Education, '74) recalls fighting her way into the School of Education after initially being told all the slots were filled and there was no room for her.

Holly Peters (Arts and Sciences, '74) decided to go to law school after determining that "lawyers could really be a force for good, for reform in

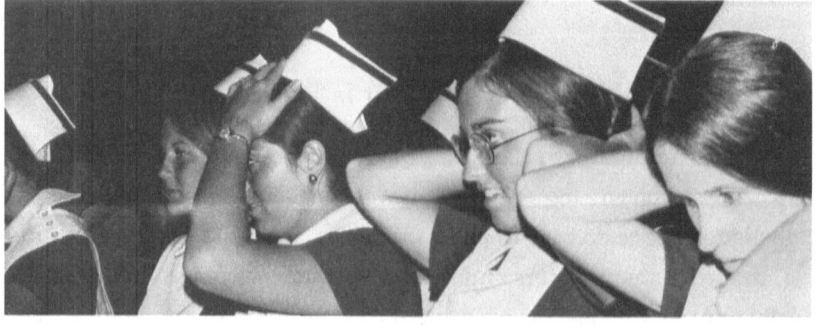

A memory-making moment for nursing students. (1974 *Corks and Curls*)

society, and that courts were a way to improve society." Several classmates indicated that their continued education and career paths stemmed from similar sentiments.

Spindrift Beck Al Swaidi spent her first two years of college at UVA. She chose the university because it was the only one in the United States that offered a five-year professional architecture degree. "I have very fond memories of my two years at UVA," she says, "though, there were clear challenges being there the first year they accepted women. For example, only four women out of 100 students were admitted to the first year of the B.A. of Architecture." While she says that the program provided "a rich learning experience," Spindrift eventually transferred to the Architectural Association in London, England, where she completed her R.I.B.A.

Alison Ingram (Engineering, '75) was one of two women who entered the School of Engineering in 1970. "The other woman student and I received comments about how she and I were there just to get husbands," she remembers. "Then she got one and didn't return second semester. So, I [became] the only woman. Some of my classmates were very gracious to me, most were indifferent, and a few made fun of me. What they didn't know is that encouraged me to try even harder."

Ingram spent five years in the program after switching from aerospace engineering to civil engineering. While more women joined the program as the years went on, she said that a program with mainly men didn't bother her. In fact, it was the reality of her work life, too, with the exception of her final engineering position.

Another gender barrier was broken in 1972 when Cynthia Goodrich (Arts and Sciences, '73) became the first woman to live on the Lawn.[16] Another woman was tapped as well, but all reports are that only Goodrich actually took up residence in a Lawn room. Living in one of the rooms that line the Lawn, in the original buildings that stood when the university opened its doors in 1825, is something that has always been considered a high honor, and today it requires a multistep application process. Gibbs reports that the desire of those first women to live on the Lawn was not without controversy. She said in a 1991 oral history interview "that there were still some of those 'old diehards,' if you will, who were anti-coeducation and said 'women can't live on the Lawn, because there are

Fourteen women in the class of 1974 lived on the
Lawn our fourth year. (1974 *Corks and Curls*)

not restrooms. It's too dark over there.' And I remember Mr. Shannon saying, 'Well, let's see what we can do about that.'"[17]

While there aren't bathrooms inside the rooms on the Lawn, Gibbs indicates that additional restrooms and showers were gradually added to accommodate women in the nearby facilities, and that lighting was improved. Fourteen of our classmates would be selected for the Lawn the following year, and some indicated that this honor was the highlight of their time at UVA.

In a variety of different ways, we continued to be "firsts." To name just a few:

—Barbara M. Golden Lynn, the first female member of the Jefferson Society
—Janet Palmer Hamel, the first female cochair of resident advisors
—Mary Bland Love, the first female business manager of the *Cavalier Daily*
—Patricia Banks, Gloria Kasey, Mary Moyer, and Barbara Savage, the first Black women to live on the Lawn
—Margaret Ann (Ann) Brown, who with former colleagues from the *Cavalier Daily*, launched a new weekly newspaper, *The Declaration*, on Founder's Day 1973

There, of course, were many other "firsts" for women in our class including memberships in honorary and secret societies, scholarships, and awards.

Dixie and the ERA

In the early 1970s, the world was changing, and so was UVA. The pep band had recently stopped playing the song "Dixie" at football games.[18] Ridding Scott Stadium, where football games were played, of the Confederate flag, however, was a trickier task. In 1971, Paulette Jones Morant (Arts and Sciences, '74) remembers the Black Student Alliance taking a petition to President Shannon to ban the Confederate flag from Grounds. "He listened to it carefully," Morant said, "and he obviously must have said something [about the flag waving], because after that it was not done unless it was done randomly by a person from the public who didn't get the memo."

The issue was not totally resolved, however, and after considerable back and forth, the administration banned all flags at the stadium.[19] First Amendment rights, states' rights, and the traditions of UVA continued to be raised as support for the Confederate flag, despite the history of slavery that the flag evoked. Confederate flags still adorned walls in fraternity houses, and themed parties celebrating the Old South would be held long after we graduated. In a picture of "The Lawn Chowder and Marching Society" from this era, several members in the front row are prominently holding the Confederate flag.[20]

The Equal Rights Amendment (ERA) was passed in 1972, but the road to ratification by the states was long and continues still. Although the state of Virginia ratified the ERA in 2021, the amendment is still entangled in legal arguments relating to the amount of time allowed for ratification and states that have voted to withdraw their votes to ratify. In 1972, Title IX of the Education Amendments also passed, amending the Civil Rights Act of 1964. It reads, "No person in the United States shall, based on sex, be excluded from participation in, be denied the benefits of, or be subjected to the discrimination under any education program or activity receiving Federal financial assistance." Title IX would have far-reaching effects on women's athletics and other academic and nonacademic issues and would make it crystal clear, for anyone still doubting, that UVA's pre-lawsuit plan, with its quota system for women's admittance, was illegal.

In 1973, *Roe v. Wade,* a landmark decision of the U.S. Supreme Court, ensured women's right to choose whether to carry a pregnancy to term. This ruling protected a woman's right to privacy under the Fourteenth Amendment of the U.S. Constitution. This decision, while giving women the constitutional rights to make decisions about their own bodies, would become one of the most divisive issues in American society. On June, 24, 2022, this right was nullified by the Supreme Court decision in *Dobbs v. Jackson Women's Health Organization.*[21] After almost fifty years of legal protection to make decisions about their bodies and health, women were now subjected to government control over their most basic and fundamental rights.

Safety Is Still an Issue

The issue of safety continued to be an issue throughout our undergraduate years. We learned to travel in groups and went to parties with a friend or two. That didn't always work well because things sometimes evolved, and our walking partner might leave early or with someone else. Many of us have memories of walking alone on dark streets, keeping to the middle of the road and hastening our pace at the smallest noise.

We also sometimes took risks that afterward we regretted. Mary Bland Love (Arts and Sciences, '74) recalls:

> I was walking on [Route] 29 back to the dorm and a car pulled over and asked me if I wanted a ride. The driver looked like a student, and I hopped in. When I told him where to turn and he didn't, I realized I had made a huge mistake. When he slowed down, I opened the door and got out. I hit the pavement and bloodied my hands and knees, but I was out of the car and that was all that mattered. It took me a long time to talk about it because I felt really stupid for getting in a car with a strange man.

There were reasons for us to feel vulnerable. Alarie Tennille (Arts and Sciences, '74) recalls the terror of her last year:

My roommate and I shared an apartment on Virginia Avenue and walked to classes. A coed was murdered in the church parking lot at the end of our block, and there was a serial rapist on the loose. The police said they knew who it was, but couldn't prove it (before DNA testing). One night I'd actually stayed alone in the apartment and went to Richmond the next morning for a job interview. When I got home, my next-door neighbor told me that [a female student who lived] next door had been raped. That, combined with my absence, had all my friends deeply worried, not to mention added to my own fears about living there.

Resident Advisors

As mentioned earlier, a number of women applied to be dorm counselors, retitled resident advisors (RAs), at the end of our first year. Some had an interest in meeting more women, and others felt that they had learned a lot about navigating UVA life and wanted to help others do the same. RAs took on a leadership role, and they contributed time to help other women. The lack of dorm space and off-Grounds housing, coupled with the expense of apartments and houses, served to make the RA program more attractive. "Women became very active as RAs," according to Gibbs. "I think they had their first impact on student life at the University through the Residence Life program."[22] It's probably not coincidental that most of the fourteen women who lived on the Lawn during our fourth year had been RAs.

The women who were tapped to become RAs knew that one area in particular demanded their attention. There was a strong need for better information about contraception, abortion, and student health services. Some of the pioneering RAs formed the Counselors Committee on Human Sexuality. Armed with pamphlets, titled "An Ounce of Prevention," repurposed from Duke University, several RAs, typically a male and female, would host dorm and suite discussions. The birth control pill was approved by the FDA in 1960, and by 1965 more than 6.5 million American women were taking oral contraceptives, making it the most popular form of birth control in the country. It was not until 1972, however, that the

U.S. Supreme Court deemed it illegal to refuse to sell the pill to an unmarried woman.

In 1972, the RAs revised and produced their own version of "An Ounce of Prevention."[23] This iteration would more explicitly explore sexuality, including homosexuality. By that time, UVA had a Gay Student Alliance, started in 1972, although a gay friend, who was several years ahead of us at UVA, reports that most of the gay students he knew, himself included, were deeply closeted during their years at the university.[24] Despite efforts to provide support, most would agree that it still was not comfortable to be gay at UVA or, for that matter, most anywhere, in the 1970s.

Expansion of Student Health Services

By our second year, a gynecologist was on duty two afternoons a week at Student Health. Dr. Ulysses (Jim) Grant Turner was a southern gentleman, if ever there was one, and also totally dedicated to providing women the health care they needed. Michele Martin arrived in Charlottesville with her husband, who was in graduate school, at the beginning of our second year. Having worked as a counselor in a health clinic in Philadelphia, she was hired by Student Health to provide counseling to the women of the UVA community.

Martin also worked with the Counselors Committee on Human Sexuality, helping to revise the materials the RAs would use when facilitating dorm discussions. She said of her time at UVA that she saw far too many women who had unprotected sex, and far too many who, she believed, had been sexually assaulted. "Sexual assault numbers were not accurate, as women often didn't report," said Martin. "Some women went to their deans, RAs, or professors who often convinced them to seek care at the Student Health Gynecology Clinic. This was all before there was a Women's Center or any UVA-sponsored group that dealt with assault."

A Difficult Reckoning

I didn't expect to include more than a passing reference to the topic of sexual assault in this book. But I made a commitment to myself to report what I heard, read, and found. In reviewing the *Cavalier Daily* for the years before and after 1970, it was clear that sexual assaults became more common for women associated with the university as the years went on or, more likely, were more often reported. Sexual abuse and assaults predated our arrival but clearly accelerated after we set foot on the Grounds. Although some changes were made to address women's safety before and during our years at UVA, the issue of sexual assault and rape would not be addressed as a priority for years to come.

In 1970, we didn't have the words or language to describe some of what we, as the first group of women, were experiencing. The empty seats beside us in classrooms, the teaching assistants and older faculty calling us Mister. The Honor Code depicted in language of the past, visibly and repeatedly. The intrusive and inappropriate questions about our personal and sexual lives and desires. In today's world, these small but consistent messages would be called microaggressions. And, we know now, these can take a toll.

While conducting research for this book, including interviewing classmates by phone and online and reading surveys conducted by other researchers, I heard and read a number of stories about sexual harassment. One classmate was crossing Beta Bridge when a guy shouted across Rugby Road, "Bitch!" Then there was a friend who returned from a mixer and described her date as growing increasingly angry as she rebuffed his advances until he gave up and told her emphatically, "You must be frigid." One housemate remembered leaving a party early, even when it meant walking the dark streets alone, after feeling uncomfortable with the behavior of the men there. Their behavior, seemingly fueled by alcohol, she told me, made her feel increasingly unsafe. Laura Wilson Small (Arts and Sciences, '74) reflected, "I learned to avoid compromising situations, but that didn't seem fair or a satisfying answer to the problem. Work still remains to be done on this issue."

In my research, I also discovered reports of behaviors that went far beyond microaggressions, that were clear aggressions, and even dangerous and criminal behavior. One account was from a woman in our class who participated in a 1985 survey. In a question about discrimination, she "spoke of an incident happening on a date during the first days of school.

'After writing on our arms and legs with black marker 'Bring Back the Old U.,' they [the students' dates] dumped us in a remote part of town. I almost left [the university] then.'"[25]

Another discrepancy between the language we have today versus then was in describing what is today known as date rape. In 1970, rape, although not defined as such, was commonly considered a violent act committed by a stranger against an unsuspecting and unprepared woman. Indeed, the *Cavalier Daily* reported several rapes prior to 1970 that were described as having been perpetrated by a non-student against a student's date, and on at least one occasion the male date was in the vicinity of the crime but reportedly was "too incapacitated" to intervene.

One classmate wrote of a sexual assault during her years at UVA that went unreported because, she said, "It was 1970." Another classmate shared the story of her roommate, who told her six months after the fact that she had been raped during Orientation Week. When I asked whether she or her roommate told anyone, she responded, "Who were you going to tell?"

Several factors spurred UVA administrators to address both the issues of sexual abuse as well as women's health. One was the number of pregnancies on the Grounds in our first years. "We were seeing at least one hundred pregnancies a year among students in those early days," said Michele Martin, who worked in the Student Health Gynecology Clinic, "and I was the options counselor for all of them." While this number is staggering given how few female students there were, it should be noted "students" included a much broader group than just our class or even undergraduates. Some were graduate students or students in the professional schools, part-time students, or students in the continuing education program, a common pathway used prior to and even after the lawsuit to admit women seeking to earn undergraduate credits.

The second factor that motivated greater involvement by the university to protect the women there is the actual reporting by female students of the crimes perpetrated against them. The "boys will be boys" sentiment or the "maybe you gave him the wrong idea about what you wanted" response, sometimes heard when women reported that they had been the victim of an assault, was becoming increasingly difficult to defend in light of the facts women presented. There would still be far more cases of abuse, assault, and rape that went unreported than were reported, for any number of reasons. Women who had been drinking at the time of the assault sometimes felt complicit in the situation. Other times the woman liked the man, or they had been dating, and this act of violence was confusing and unexpected. Sometimes the woman felt she wouldn't be believed, and often women didn't want to face what they knew would be fraught next steps. History has shown us time and time again that it is often not the perpetrators but the women who are victims of assault who are shamed. And, in an inexplicable turn of logic, women are often blamed—for where they were, what they wore, if and how much they drank, or even who they were with—for example, attending a party and being in the presence of a man with violent, abusive plans. And it isn't surprising that women often felt responsible. In a December 12, 1972, article in the *Cavalier Daily* titled "Security Seminar Advises Women in Proper Means of Self Defense," it was reported that in the session sponsored by the first-year and upperclass resident staffs, "women were cautioned against teasing men and urged to be careful in what they say and wear in the classroom. Bra-less attire, see-through blouses and short mini-skirts were labeled taboo for the classroom."

Incremental Progress

The university would make incremental gains in addressing women's issues and concerns, including women's autonomy, safety, and security. Gibbs insisted female students be called "women," not "girls." Call boxes would be installed, safe escort services employed, better lighting constructed across Grounds. Women would begin talking about what they expected and required in terms of respectful and appropriate behavior, and men were beginning to be schooled in boundaries. This situation wasn't resolved during our tenure at UVA, and there is still today much work to be done, but it was a start.

The student council organized a Women's Committee, and Kevin Mannix (Arts and Sciences, '71; Law, '74) related that dorm talks became part of the committee's work. In 1979, plans were made to start a women's studies program. Sharon Davie, an English professor and UVA alumna, created a curriculum, and in 1988, the program began offering majors.[26] In 1989, after the university community petitioned the administration, Davie became the first director of UVA's Women's Center, which opened with the vision of "fostering leadership, engaged scholarship, safety, and well-being."[27] The name was changed in 2014 to the Maxine Platzer Lynn Women's Center after an alumna pledged an endowment to support the ongoing work of the center.

Four Years Fly By

Most of us would walk the Lawn on May 19, 1974, in Final Exercises (another UVA term, this one for "graduation") on a glorious sunny morning. Edgar Shannon, retiring later that summer, would give our commencement speech. George Allen (Arts and Sciences, '74; Law, '77), who would later become the governor of Virginia and a U.S. senator, said that in his position as president of the graduating class he helped make the decision about speakers. He recounted that he "insisted students be polled for the Baccalaureate speaker, resulting in the selection of Garry Trudeau," of *Doonesbury* comic strip fame, a nontraditional pick by most anyone's estimation. Allen said having Edgar Shannon serve as commencement speaker was an easy decision.

Shannon would resume his teaching life in the English department, where he, like most UVA administrators, had continued to teach a class (on Tennyson) during our tenure. He said, reflecting on his years as UVA's president, that shepherding the coeducation process at the university was one of his greatest accomplishments. Some felt his retirement might have been accelerated, in part, by the combination of the May Day Strike and coeducation and the vocal alumni discontent around both.[28] Just as fifty years earlier President Alderman reportedly had lost favor by pushing for a coordinate college to serve women, Shannon may have suffered a similar fate.

Many of us would leave the Grounds and Charlottesville for our next chapter later that day. Some would stay on for work, or to begin graduate or professional school. Many of us would cry as we were leaving, recognizing that we would likely never be as carefree again. Years later, Liz McLeod (Arts and Sciences, '74) reflected, "I would say that the people and the beauty of the Grounds are what I think of when I tell people about why I loved UVA."

After graduation, I was off to Ft. Lee, New Jersey, and a job in publishing in New York City. Larry and I were married in the university chapel the day before Final Exercises. The wedding was timed so that we could include our families from Michigan and New York and, just as importantly, our UVA friends who for more than three years had watched and supported our love. Our vision of a big party in lieu of a stuffy reception was realized that Saturday afternoon in May. There was dancing and singing and our friends commandeering the mic, becoming the impromptu entertainment. Forty-five years later when a Florida hurricane destroyed our wedding album, I would reconnect with Ed Roseberry, who was our wedding photographer and the chronicler of UVA athletics and parties for more than forty years. Despite being in his nineties, he searched through the files he had donated to UVA's archives—the same archives that would yield much of the backstory for this book. He found the negatives, digitized them, and sent them to me. Just one more UVA story for the record books!

SIX

TRAILBLAZERS AND PIONEERS

Women belong in all places where decisions are being made.
—Ruth Bader Ginsburg

PHIL SCHLECHTY, A FRIEND of mine and founder of the Center for Leadership in School Reform in Louisville, Kentucky, now the Schlechty Center, believed in the power of story as a vehicle of change. He also happened to be a great storyteller. He passed away in 2016, but he spent his professional life working to improve the public school system. When he spoke to audiences, he would transport them back to frosty Ohio mornings, when as a child he sat next to his father in his dad's milk truck, making deliveries. He just as vividly described what it was like to try to implement change in seemingly intractable school faculties who seemed satisfied with, and who carefully guarded, the status quo.

If you were an educator during the past fifty years, you've likely read Schlechty's work or heard him speak. When attempting to get school leaders to "sign on" to his "working on the work," a strategy for improving the quality of student work, he identified five roles that participants played in the process: trailblazers, pioneers, settlers, stay-at-homes, and saboteurs. Schlechty would say that being a trailblazer or a pioneer was a tough duty—but you couldn't effect change without people in these roles. Every change effort, he would argue, required courageous and brave trailblazers and pioneers.[1]

Using Schlechty's metaphor, UVA's coeducation journey was composed of both—women who were trailblazers and those who were pioneers. Virginia Scott and Cynthia Goodrich, who was the first woman to live on the Lawn, were definitely trailblazers, forging a previously untrodden path. And the 668 undergraduate women who arrived at UVA in 1970—367 of whom were starting their first year of college—can aptly be called pioneers. Indeed, many of those women and others who were part of their journey—including administrators, male students, and professors—call this the class of "pioneering women."

After graduation, women in our class continued to break molds, challenge the status quo, and become leaders in their communities and career fields. Attorneys of all stripes, doctors and nurses of all specialties, teachers, school administrators and professors, along with writers, poets, publishers, small business owners, accountants, government analysts, actors, artists, and judges. Some classmates believe their most significant contribution and life's work is not what they've done, but who they have raised.

There is little question, individually and collectively, that this is an accomplished group of women. Below is a "snapshot" of a few women who serve as proxies for the trailblazing and pioneering women who transformed UVA.

Virginia A. (Ginger) Scott

> I feel fortunate to have had the opportunity to be a part of this suit and to watch it unfold. I am grateful for the outcome which enabled me to receive an education that enriched my life across many dimensions.
>
> —Virginia A. Scott

Although she had to battle her way in, once there, Virginia A. (Ginger) Scott made it quite clear she belonged at UVA. Graduating with a degree in religious studies with honors, she went on to complete two graduate degrees—one in the College of Arts and Sciences in 1980 and one in the School of Education in 1989. Virginia's journey to matriculation at UVA was a difficult and roundabout one. She graduated from Albemarle High

School in Charlottesville in 1968. She left the College of William and Mary during her first semester to care for her mother in Charlottesville. After her mother died, she was glad to work for a young attorney, John Lowe, who had recently completed his law degree at UVA.

When a discussion ensued about her college plans, Lowe suggested she attend UVA. Virginia responded that UVA didn't admit undergraduate women in the College of Arts and Sciences.[2] Lowe wasn't aware of that, an interesting admission from an alumnus of the law school, but perhaps indicative of the divisions between professional schools, where women were students, albeit in small numbers, and the undergraduate programs of the college. Lowe had worked with the ACLU on other cases, and as he recalled in *UVA Today*, he responded, "Well, then, we'll just have to take care of that," and he got to work.[3]

Reportedly, with the help of Mary Whitney, the dean of women at the time, Lowe recruited three other female students to request UVA application materials, knowing they would not be offered the opportunity to apply to the undergraduate program in the College of Arts and Sciences. Dean Ern met with Scott, who, based on the notes he took on her interview form, indicated that if she wasn't offered a chance to apply for a place in the college, she would file suit with the help of the ACLU.[4] Armed with clear evidence that based on gender, the four women were denied the ability to apply for admission, on May 29, 1969, Lowe and his ACLU colleagues sued the university in federal court in Richmond.

A temporary injunction was issued in late September, prior to the court date, allowing Scott to attend classes in the college during the fall 1969 term. Scott reports a mixed response from the men in attendance, who, had they been unaware of the court case, were reminded in an article in the *Cavalier Daily* on October 1, 1969. The headline read, "Coed Admittance to College Forced by Court Injunction." The article reported that Scott was "one of two girls enrolled as a first-year undergraduate in the College of Arts and Sciences"; the other was the unnamed wife of a faculty member. The article continues, "The series of events which has culminated in the acceptance of Miss Scott into the previously all-male College has been long and involved, and the present situation is by no means final. But for now, the fact remains that Miss Scott is in the College, she is registered for a normal course schedule, and she is attending classes."

Virginia Scott was a true hero. (*Cavalier Daily*, October 3, 1969)

On October 3, the *Cavalier Daily* would do another front-page story about Scott, complete with three photographs and the label "suffragette":

> When the suffragette was asked in an interview with the *Cavalier Daily* about the decision of the judges, she confessed "I'm reluctant to even comment on that. If I look at it from my viewpoint, I'm disappointed because I would have liked them to have decided on the question of constitutionality. But if I look at it from the judges' viewpoint, then I can understand why they want more time. I might not be so sympathetic after the final hearing."

When I interviewed Scott for this book, I asked her how her path to matriculation and attendance at UVA informed her later life. "I switched from Religious Studies to Education, working between the two while I put money together for another degree," she said. "I had hoped to get a Ph.D. but forecasts for academic jobs were grim. I returned to the work world until I heard about a new program in the Ed School in Instructional Design."

Instructional Design and Technology is a program that teaches professionals how to create curriculum using a variety of technology. At the time, it was a new field, and Scott found the mix of science and art fascinating.

"After I completed the M.Ed., I worked for UVA's School of Continuing Education as a designer and videographer for a distance education program for reading teachers," said Scott. After ten years, she left and began freelancing as an instructional designer helping colleges and universities reconfigure courses for online delivery.

Now, looking back, Scott can clearly see the through line between her history-making, path-forging lawsuit and what became her life's work. "Designing online courses was a natural continuation of my dedication to helping make a college education available to underserved students that began with my participation in the lawsuit against UVA," she says. "Single parents who had to keep working while going to school, military personnel serving overseas, older students who wanted to return to college after their children were college educated but needed to work full-time, and people living in remote areas without institutions of higher learning nearby were able to fulfill their dreams because of online courses and degree programs. Also, in the big picture, our democracy depends on an educated citizenry and online education increases the opportunity for people to further their education."

Scott, a true trailblazer, made her mark on Mr. Jefferson's university. Carla Williams, the first Black female athletic director at UVA, once remarked, "Sometimes it's just easier to be second."[5] Easier, yes, but someone has to be first. Scott continues to live in the Charlottesville area. A plaque erected in front of Peabody Hall pays tribute to her role in the lawsuit that was a major piece of UVA's coeducational journey.

Barbara M. Golden Lynn

> Throughout all of that time, as a lawyer and judge, I've used... knowledge, wisdom and tenacity... to fight for ideas to become reality, to help to achieve justice, and to promote fairness and equity.
> —Barbara M. Golden Lynn

On a sunny afternoon in September 1970, Barbara M. Golden Lynn's parents said goodbye in the parking lot after helping her move into her dorm. Barbara had never seen the UVA Grounds, nor had she ever been to Charlottesville. She selected UVA as an honors student at Miami Norland High School in Miami Gardens, Florida, based on reputation and cost, not

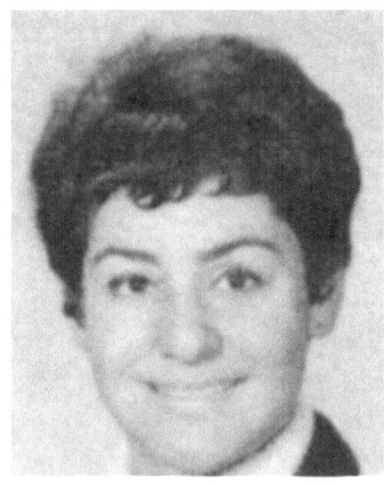

Barbara M. Golden Lynn. (*The First Year Directory of the Class of 1974*)

wanting her college expenses to be too much of a burden on her parents. "I was standing in the road outside and my parents drove away," Barbara said. "I had really never been away from home at all. My parents had never visited the University before I went there to go to school, and I was crying and thinking, 'I don't know a soul.'"

Barbara was an Echols scholar, which means she was a member of the Honors Program in UVA's College of Arts and Sciences. Fortunately, Echols scholars, who are housed together, had a faculty member assigned to the group who lived in their dorm. Charlie Whitebread, a law professor held in high esteem as a scholar and all-around nice guy, was assigned to Barbara's group of Echols scholars. "Charlie Whitebread was brilliant and crazy and fun," said Barbara, "and the perfect person to take someone like me under his wing and push [the group of] us out of the nest." Barbara says the community of scholars helped her acclimate, and soon she was going out and enjoying Charlottesville. Watson Dorm housed the other approximately sixteen female Echols scholars and the greater number of male students in the program, as well as some nonprogram students.

Barbara met Mike Lynn, the man who quickly became her boyfriend, and later her husband, early in her first year. Interested in the Jefferson Literary and Debating Society, she attended meetings with Mike, who was a third-year student and a member. She applied to join, was interviewed, and then was promptly rejected, as the Jefferson Society's bylaws stated members had to be male. Her second year she would interview again, referring to the interview questions on the *Gritty Women* podcast as "extremely vulgar."[6]

When asked if those kinds of questions, perhaps meant to embarrass and demean her, made her less interested in being a member, she responded, "I knew what they were doing. The first year in Jeff Society you're on probation and you have to prove yourself to become a member—they would interrupt you and ask off-topic questions to see how you would react on your feet. So, the interview was meant, in some ways, to see how you would do with that."

In what some would label a coup—and others would indicate was just brilliant strategy—Mike Lynn saw an opportunity to affect change, and he seized it. Mike, who was vice president of the society, was temporarily operating as president while the president and a number of members, who Mike later called "the anti-women cabal," were in New Orleans for Mardi Gras. During that time, he held a vote to change the bylaws, and Barbara, who had already interviewed, was immediately voted in. Her picture hangs in Jefferson Hall as the first female member. She is quick, though, to give Mike credit.[7]

Mike, a Texan, would leave for law school at Southern Methodist University (SMU) in Dallas in 1972. He and Barbara evaluated the challenge of maintaining a long-distance relationship. "I knew we could survive one year apart, but I thought it was very unlikely we would survive two," Barbara said. "I took my credits that I came in with and I went to summer school and graduated in three years. It was for personal reasons, and I wish I didn't have to do it because I loved going to school at UVA."

Mike and Barbara married the summer of 1973, and she joined him at SMU. Barbara, not surprisingly, graduated first in her law class at SMU, but she and her other female classmates, also at the top of the class, were not getting job offers. "The law firms in Dallas were discriminating against women and we [Barbara and women in her class] decided to sue them," she said. "I think had it not been for [my] experience [at UVA], of needing to knock down barriers and not just going around them, I probably would not have been the person I was or have had the intestinal fortitude to go through that." The women sued most of the major law firms, and most settled, changing their hiring practices.

Barbara became the first female lawyer at Carrington Coleman, a large Dallas firm, and remained there for twenty-three years. In late 1998, President Bill Clinton nominated her to serve on the U.S. District Court for the Northern District of Texas, and she was confirmed a year later. She became chief judge in May 2016, the first woman to hold the position. In April 2023, Barbara notified President Biden that she would like to be moved to senior status and began serving in that capacity May 15 of that year. In typical Barbara fashion, she kept a very active caseload.

Barbara conducted Zoom conferences and meetings during the COVID-19 pandemic and held a jury trial, with all kinds of safety features, in June 2020, believing that it was important to keep legal proceedings as public as possible, even during those challenging days.

Barbara was part of a forum for the Dallas Bar Association in 2018, where she talked about the gray areas of decision making:

> Many cases fall 51–49. I don't think the nuance of the law is something people are comfortable with. I think no one knows, if you're not in the legal field, that there isn't a big book that we look in to find every answer. Most cases that come to court provide interesting issues that arise from the law that we know, but the law that we know is not immediately dispositive of the issue presented. And we must reason to a result through the law, and it's often not a straight path to get there. I don't think most people understand that.[8]

In August 2021, Barbara was the inaugural recipient of the Dallas Bar Association Jurist of the Year award, henceforth known as the Barbara M. G. Lynn Jurist of the Year Award. The award "was established to honor judges who make significant contributions to the legal community in North Texas and demonstrate high ideals, exemplary personal character, and judicial competence." Barbara, who has spoken in public forums about term limits for Supreme Court justices, intends to retire from her position in 2025. "I will have been a judge for 25 years, which I think is as long as I should serve," she said. "I want to make room for someone else, and I don't want to get stale, and I think that's enough. It will be time for someone else to take over."⁹

Barbara and Mike give back generously with their time and talents to their Dallas community and are especially dedicated to assisting younger attorneys. They both travel to Charlottesville as much as they can, meeting with scholarship applicants and visiting professors who have remained lifelong friends. They have a second home in New Mexico, where they retreat with their daughters and grandchildren. One daughter and her family live in California, and the other lives with her family in New Mexico.

Barbara sees her daughters and grandchildren as often as she can considering she happens to have a pretty important day job.

Frances Dickinson (Dickie) McMullan

> One of the benefits of getting on in years is that one is less likely to get blind-sided. Good surprises are just that. So, my mission now is the pursuit of awe and wonderment.
> —Frances Dickinson (Dickie) McMullan

Thomas Jefferson is often described as a Renaissance man, and if ever there were an example of a Renaissance woman, it would be Frances Dickinson (Dickie) McMullan. Trying to pin Dickie (the name she was called from birth) down for interviews required navigating around her extensive work obligations and travel. In the span of six months, Dickie would study French in Provence (a bucket list goal to achieve fluency), explore the art and architecture of Paris (where she'd forego hotels and reside in an apartment to better integrate into the community) and scuba dive and bird-watch on the island of St. Lucia.

Dickie was the daughter, granddaughter, and niece of physicians, and at an early age, she began showing interest in the manual dexterity and precision needed as a surgeon. In particular, she enjoyed a type of needlework known as crewel embroidery, which uses wool. Then she became interested in light and refraction after writing a physics paper on the topics—and the seeds were sown for pursuing ophthalmic surgery as a

Dickie McMullan. (Courtesy of Dickie McMullan)

profession. Following her UVA graduation, Dickie attended the Medical College of Virginia in Richmond. She did her ophthalmology residency at Emory University and Grady Hospital, a Cornea Fellowship at Tufts New England Medical Center, and then a second fellowship to learn an evolving cataract surgical procedure with lens implantation and laser surgery in the Atlanta practice of one of the procedure's innovators. This cutting-edge eye surgeon would become her professional partner, and husband of twenty years, until his death in 2003.

Growing up in the shadows of the Virginia capital and historic homes on Monument Avenue in Richmond, and visiting the European capitals in 1967, Dickie had been captivated by architecture. As a Lawn resident, she "had, on a daily basis, the opportunity to revel in the classical design, scale, symmetry and beauty of Jefferson's Academical Village." Later, when the inevitable need arose to expand and update facilities, Dickie sat on the Grounds Committee of the College Foundation Board as they wrestled with the dichotomy of preserving UVA's historic and classical beauty while addressing the university's growth.

As a student, Dickie worked hard and played hard, and her sense of adventure and infectious laugh made her a lot of fun to be around. She recalls a meeting with Dean Ern her first week at UVA, and it didn't have anything to do with admissions. Instead, Dickie remembers "sitting across from Dean Ern explaining why I was in the heating tunnels under the University as discovered by a UCop." Despite breaking the rules to explore the Grounds' crisscrossing network of underground tunnels, which house steam pipes, Dickie was one of the women Ernie Ern remembered fondly when I interviewed him about our class fifty years later.

Dickie worked on the *Corks and Curls* yearbook, served as a resident advisor, and, in her third year, was elected to the Judiciary Council. The summer of 1973 she was the first female College of Arts and Sciences student to serve in an Honor Committee Trial. She played coed water polo in Mem Gym's basement pool and was a cheerleader with the first cadre of women from our class. And even though the NCAA does not recognize cheerleading as a sport, I can't help but think that Dickie would have made a fortune with today's NIL (name, image, and likeness) platform. Dickie has always been a presence, and in today's world of Instagram, X (formerly Twitter), and 24/7 media, it's not hard to imagine her popping up on our phones to remind us that The Virginian still has the best sandwiches on the Corner.

As an eye surgeon in Atlanta, Dickie continues to help patients maintain and improve their vision into her eighth decade. As in so many professions in the 1970s, medicine in general, and surgery in particular, were male-dominated. The resilience and perseverance required to navigate the rigors of this fraternity were honed in Dickie's undergraduate years at UVA.

Dickie recalls, "The community at UVA provided, for me, a safe place to explore options, make decisions, and live with the consequences, good or not-so-good. My affiliation and identity with the accomplished founder, alumni, faculty, and classmates gave me a sense of belonging and confidence, adding to a foundation that gave me my sea-legs for the next part of my journey."

"Giving back" has also afforded Dickie the opportunity to quench some wanderlust. She has taken mission trips to countries in need of even the most basic ophthalmic attention, including clinical work in Bhutan, the Fiji Islands, and Tanzania, where her nephew Hunter Flint (Arts and Sciences, '06) ran a coffee plantation. She traveled with other medical personnel to Madagascar and the highlands of Papua New Guinea, performing intra-ocular surgery on patients in need of her skills.

Dickie is the eldest of four daughters and aunt to three nieces, all UVA alumnae, and her sorority continues to be her sisters and nieces, her UVA pals, and her enlarging circle of friends. She is consciously making decisions that allow her to be more available to her friends and to spend more time with them. As Dickie's next chapter unfolds, she anticipates continued awe and wonder. (You can see more from Dr. Dickie McMullan at youtube.com.)

Paulette Jones Morant

> As soon as we got out of the car and saw the Rotunda, we said, "This is it!" And that's how the love affair with UVA really began. When I saw the Lawn and the Rotunda I said, "I can't believe I'm going here."
> —Paulette Jones Morant

When Paulette, who was commonly called P.J. while she was a student at UVA, joined the online chat during the live ReTold event in October 2020, there was an immediate burst of activity. Energized by her presence, classmates excitedly started greeting her and asking questions. Paulette is one of those people who "never met a stranger." Even though she describes herself as somewhat shy ("Being the first one to say 'hello' is hard for me . . . even though I'm a talker"), she also is genuinely curious about new people and enthusiastic about new experiences. It was her innate curiosity that led her to participate in sports at UVA, something that she had only done during gym class in high school. And reluctantly at that.

During 2022, the fiftieth reunion of the passage of Title IX (the amendment to the Higher Education Act banning sex-based discrimination in education programs receiving federal funding), the stories of Paulette's involvement in the first club sports and later intercollegiate sports were featured in several media outlets. The article "'Accidental Athlete' Helped Lead the Way for Women, Black Students in Early '70s" written by Jeff White was featured in *UVA Today* online on March 17, 2022. It states that Morant, then a second-year student, had a friend who invited her to tag along to a field hockey club meeting. The friend mentioned there would be someone there from New Zealand who was going to tell them all about field hockey.

Paulette Jones Morant.
(1974 *Corks and Curls*)

Morant is quoted as having replied, "I actually hate that game. I don't get it. But I do want to meet this kid from New Zealand, so I'll come with you." The article continues, "At the meeting, Morant discussed her aversion to the sport with a graduate student who was organizing the club, "and she said, 'Oh, I can make you like it.' I went, 'All right, I want to see you do it.'"

Field hockey became an intercollegiate sport Paulette's fourth year, and she also managed the first women's club basketball team her second and third years. She spoke of these experiences with Doria Martingayle on October 18, 2022, for "Sabre TV," a UVA-centered sports program. In the video, which is available on YouTube, she speaks about these experiences as well as how at times she felt like she and other women were a "curiosity" on Grounds, but, she clarifies, personally, she never felt disdained. She also is featured in a short film, *Accidental Athlete*, codirected by Claudrena Harold and Kevin Jerome Everson, which was screened at the Virginia Film Festival on November 4, 2022.[10]

Paulette describes her years at UVA as a time of saying "yes" to everything. She and her suitemate Vivian Lerner, neither with a background in broadcasting or music, launched a radio program on WTJU featuring classical music, and it was on the air for three and a half years. Paulette, like most African American students at UVA, joined Black Students for

Freedom, renamed in her second year as the Black Student Alliance (BSA). She believes, she says, that this organization gave the few Black students on Grounds a community that provided social, emotional, and political support. In the fall of 1971, she recalls signing a petition against UVA's traditional waving of the Confederate flag after touchdowns at Scott Stadium football games. She then marched with other Black students to President Shannon's office to present it to him. Paulette noted that President Shannon's response was to ban all flags at the football stadium.

In our interview, Paulette acknowledged that it was at times challenging to be one of the few women on Grounds, and one of even fewer Black women. She suggested, too, that the UVA experience may have been harder for those Black students at UVA who had previously attended segregated high schools, which she had not. She also recognized how hard it likely was for some of the Black male students who were often stopped on Grounds by the university police and required to show them their student ID.

After earning her master's in Spanish at The Ohio State University, in 1980 Paulette married Blake Morant, a double Hoo, which means Blake earned two degrees from UVA, and taught high school Spanish for many years. Her enthusiasm for teaching turned into a love of connecting people, often through her passion for photography. She and Blake help organize the Black Alumni Weekends, support the Ridley Scholarship, and are steadfast in their efforts to help UVA realize its potential and become a more inclusive university. They were recognized in the 2022 Alumni Development magazine for their financial commitment to the university.[11]

Paulette's love of people—and her love of life—are evident in everything she does. She organized "The Culture Vultures," a small group of women living in northern Virginia, most of whom are from our class, who get together regularly to enjoy the museums and restaurants of Washington, D.C. She loves to travel and hopes in the years ahead to make that a priority.

She is proud of her award-winning photography, which continues to be a source of joy for her. She says:

> I've had some success in having works shown in local exhibitions in my hometown area of Hampton Roads, Virginia. It has taken some time to

consider myself an artist, but I now feel comfortable doing so, realizing the many levels and variations of photographic art. My most memorable artistic experience was my first solo photography exhibition, held in Lexington, Virginia in 2023. I am very grateful that friends, family and visitors to the gallery shared joy in my perspectives.

Paulette is not slowing down. If anything, she is busier than ever, with so much to discover and so many people to meet and with whom to connect. Her UVA years of saying "yes" were just a prelude for the years to follow. And that's not accidental.

Barbara Savage

> As in most of life, people and relationships matter in getting anything done within institutions.
>
> —Barbara Savage

Barbara Savage grew up in Southampton, Virginia, the daughter of working-class parents who had not attended college. She was also one of the small group of Black women who entered UVA in September 1970. In 2021, Barbara moderated a webinar, "The Women of 1974," a follow-up to the ReTold summit, and spoke about how she decided to apply to and attend UVA:

> I think that's one of the virtues of being young and just sort of cast into something. At the time, you may not know the full significance of it. I graduated from the last all-Black high school in my county—the next year, the school system was going to be integrated. But my class was segregated and all Black. We were part of that Civil Rights generation—we were too young to be in the movement, but we were brought up with the notion of taking advantage of every opportunity that the movement opened for us. I think that we saw everything that had gone on—if we were born in the mid 50s and with television, we were very well aware of all the assassinations, all the folks in the street protesting for Civil Rights, but also the Vietnam War protests, which had started in the late 60s and early 70s. And so, I think there was, for me at least as a young Black person who had been raised with

the notion that education is the key, there was the sense that you step in and you take advantage of this opportunity. There was also this notion that my parents and my grandparents and all the Black people I knew in rural Virginia, had been paying taxes all these years and Black people could not go to the University. So there was also this sense that this is a public school and we've been supporting it, and so yes, we must step in and take advantage of that opportunity.

Barbara spoke in the November 2021 webinar about what it was like being among so few Black students. "I think that it took me about ten years after I left UVA to figure out how alienating it was," she said.

I got there, I met people I liked, I focused on my classes, I joined the pep band, and—I'm quite reserved. I would say I'm probably an introvert. For people who were more socially oriented, who would have wanted to have a more typical kind of college social life, I imagine that it would have been much more difficult in a way. I wasn't really looking for that and so I didn't

Barbara Savage and classmates. (Courtesy of Barbara Savage)

miss it. I did have a nice cohort of friends, some of whom I'm still really close with, so I think that's also part of it. It depends on temperament and personality ... and I came with a really strong sense of purpose and mission and this idea that this was a new educational opportunity. And I felt some broader responsibilities to represent both Black women and the Black community more generally. I did not experience that as a burden at the time; I saw it as I was ready to take advantage of the opportunity. I felt like I had been born too late to participate in the Civil Rights movement, a generation shy of that, and the sacrifices that so many people—Black and white—made, [were] for the kinds of opportunities I had.

Barbara credits her Black high school teachers with giving her a strong educational foundation and "a real strong sense of confidence," which she said was very important to her success at UVA. "I was immediately surrounded by women in my dorm who had had all sorts of opportunities that had never come my way," she said, "and to be able to still be grounded in my own self and to succeed, I think, was very affirming."

When asked about the first weeks, when, a white classmate observed, fraternities were hand-delivering invitations to white women but not Black women, Barbara said:

> I wouldn't have been interested in that even if I had gone to a different school, where things like that would have been open to us. And I have to say, things were not that difficult for me because I came with a male classmate from high school, and he was a really good friend. We also had a friend who was a year ahead of us in the Engineering school, so the three of us would drive back and forth to UVA, and that made all the difference in the world. I knew their families and they gave my parents a great deal of comfort that I wasn't up there by myself, and in that way, it was a little community.

Barbara's career path has had a few twists and turns, all of which she said led her to discovering what she really wanted to do. Barbara continued her education with a law degree from Georgetown University. "I saw law as the best way to serve the social justice issues I wanted to be part of," she said. "I saw these examples of the heroic work by lawyers, Black and white, during the Civil Rights movement, but I was never drawn to a traditional law practice or to be a litigator."

Barbara enjoyed policy work and writing position papers, and her work at the Children's Defense Fund allowed her to work on issues related to Black families. She began taking graduate courses in history at George Mason University. "I basically convinced myself that it would not be turning my back on political commitments if I decided that my place was to basically read research and write and teach," she said, "and that's the sense of mission I took with me when I decided to go to Graduate School." Barbara received her doctorate in history from Yale in 1995. Remarkably, during graduate school, she served as director of federal relations in the Office of the General Counsel at Yale University.

Barbara is currently the Geraldine R. Segal Professor Emerita of American Social Thought and Professor Emeritus for Africana Studies at the University of Pennsylvania. She has written books exploring the intersection of religion and politics, and when we spoke, she was working on a biography of Vernie Merze Tate, *Merze Tate: The Global Odyssey of a Black Woman Scholar,* which was published in the fall of 2023. Tate was a professor, scholar, and expert in U.S. diplomacy. "She was a willful woman who was born in 1905 and died in 1996," Barbara said. "Her life permits me as a scholar to think about the entirety of the twentieth century, especially around issues related to race, gender, and education."

I considered it a great feat when I extracted a promise, of sorts, from Barbara that she would write a young adult version of the Tate biography for me to share with my grandchildren.

Alarie Tennille

> I'm a UVA pioneer coed with a BA in English, a Phi Beta Kappa key, and a black belt in feminism.
> —Alarie Tennille

Alarie Tennille was born and raised in Portsmouth, Virginia. A self-described shy, visually impaired young woman, Alarie always considered herself a feminist. After all, her mother had been a member of the WAVES unit in World War II, Women Accepted for Voluntary Emergency Service, and raised her to be strong and independent. After graduating from UVA, Alarie began working as a copyeditor at a law publishing house in Charlottesville. When she realized the discrepancy in pay between the male employees and female employees, she became more of an activist. "The firm hired a lot of young female attorneys (i.e., they could save money)," Alarie said, "and from them I learned about the new NOW chapter being launched and joined a consciousness-raising group. As a result, I also began to crusade for the Equal Rights Amendment." Her poem, "She Doesn't Have to Call Me Bitch," tells of an actual event from her life when Alarie and an older man were at a NOW table at Barracks Road Shopping Center, handing out literature about the ERA.

She Doesn't Have to Call Me a Bitch

Everything about her
shouts it—the red face, bared
teeth, the way she charges
like a shrieking hyena. Ignoring
the older man beside me, she singles
me out for the kill. "YOU
are destroying the family!"
she screams. Hoisting a sweaty
baby like a trophy, she sputters,
"MY daughter is going to be a LADY!"

I sit at an outdoor table, spread
with N.O.W. pamphlets and petitions
for the Equal Rights Amendment.
I look her in the eye, say nothing,
become a wall that her words
bounce off. She turns on her heel,
huffs away.

The silence sizzles.

—Alarie Tennille, first published in *Gimme Your Lunch Money: Heartland Poets Speak Out against Bullies*

Alarie's path to UVA was predictable as sibling rivalry goes. Her older brother, whom she referred to then, and continues to refer to today, as

Alarie Tennille. (1974 *Corks and Curls*)

her "genius brother," attended UVA, graduating in 1969, and told her she couldn't go there. So, of course, once she could, that's where she wanted to go. There's a little more to the story than proving her brother wrong. She visited as a teen and fell in love with the "aura, the appearance, the ambience." She loved the history of the university and knew UVA had a renowned English department. Alarie discovered a love of language and writing after her parents said they wouldn't support a college education if she majored in art. She excelled academically in high school (salutatorian), although not a poet then or at UVA. As a first-year student, she wrote a humorous mock-Shakespearean play with parts for her close friends as a Christmas gift. She also took a creative writing class (though the university didn't yet have a strong writing program).

After Alarie left the law publishing house, she took a position as a technical editor with Old Dominion University Research Foundation. The work and pay were a bit better—she reports she "had a private office and water view of an inlet." Four and a half years later, she moved with her husband, Chris Purcell (Arts and Sciences, '74), who was also an English major, to Kansas City, Missouri. Chris had been teaching English at Virginia Beach Junior High when he received a job offer from Hallmark Cards. Alarie initially stayed behind to sell their house, and during that time her mother died unexpectedly. "Things got really rough then," Alarie said. She had strong ties to the coast and Virginia, but ultimately she would head off to Missouri to join her new husband. Alarie received a job offer from Hallmark, and after a few years working as an editor, she realized that writing the card copy would enable her to satisfy at least some of her creative side. So she became a writer, crafting her own poetry on the side. Because of her work at Hallmark, she was able to attend classes and seminars with visiting poets, which helped her keep at her own writing and grow as a poet.

Alarie doesn't write poetry for the money. If she depended on it for that, she says, she would likely starve. She and Chris both retired in 2012, taking early retirement packages from Hallmark "that were too good to refuse." She has more time these days for her own writing and giving poetry readings, something she now enjoys, after overcoming earlier stage fright. (To see more of her poetry and her blogs on overcoming stage fright, visit https://www.alariepoet.com.)

Taking Forever One Day at a Time

To Chris

I love

the way you return from errands
with a present—a Danish, book, or bottle
of champagne

how you thank me for every meal
from coq au vin to a ham sandwich
and make coworkers think
I'm Julia Child

hearing your voice in conversation
downstairs before realizing
that you're talking to the cats
in the same serious tone you use
with plumbers

how you told me I was funny long before
anyone else did

that time in France when I said our waiter
looked like Orlando Bloom and you answered
then we'll have to come back tomorrow

the fun of reading a book you've just finished
and finding *oops! duh!* or *what a jerk!*
penciled in the margin

the way you reach for my hand
before crossing the street

how you describe every dark-eyed
brunette—she looks like you—no matter
how silver I go.

No wonder forty years have sneaked by.
          —Alarie Tennille, first published in *Minute Magazine*

In 2021, Alarie went back to her hometown for a delayed fiftieth high school reunion, writing "Home Coming" as a gift to her class. She still loves the water and the marshy areas and the smell and feel of her childhood. And like a lot of us who have returned "home," she found it was no longer there.

Home Coming

To go back to your hometown
and find it doesn't recognize you.

To see your old house bedraggled
like hand-me-downs left to Goodwill–

gutters stripped, azaleas gone for no good
reason except it's not your home.

To dread awkward reunions almost as much
as not running into anyone you know.

To get a little lost, finding landmarks
have run away with your childhood.

To startle at the silver-haired man
walking by who's too much like your dad.

To feel gutted by the gap that was
your high school, but jealous

of a new museum and elegant restaurants
where you'll never have a favorite table.

To understand this strange place
doesn't feel like home, but always will be.
—Alarie Tennille, first published in *Poetry Breakfast*

SEVEN

THE WORLD WE'RE LIVING INTO

> It took me quite a long time to develop a voice, and now that I have it, I am not going to be silent.
>
> —Madeleine Albright

I BEGAN RESEARCHING THIS BOOK in 2019, and in early 2020 during the COVID-19 pandemic I also began teaching my three grandchildren over Zoom. I remember helping my granddaughter study Ancient Rome and learning together about Janus, the God of doors and transitions. He had a face in two directions and could look forward and backward simultaneously. It struck me as an apt metaphor for the journey I undertook in writing this book: the doors that opened as I searched the archives to find the backstory to accounts I'd heard and often had wrong. So many conversations about those significant years in Charlottesville as we grew into adults and what that means for us as women today. Janus also serves as a metaphor for what it was like as the first class of undergraduate women. We were looking forward to a more inclusive, equitable future, while also forced to navigate the traditions and beliefs of the past.

Our Legacy

I've done my best in this book to present the facts I've found through extensive research and interviews. But, of course, our history is not just fixed words on paper, it is not just one succinct story. It is a compilation of rich, multidimensional lived experiences. It's our memories, our opinions, our felt sense of those times. And no one way of presenting that will ever get it all the way right or represent everyone's vantage point.

I also anticipate that when key administrators, currently the keeper of their files and other documents, pass those along to the archives, there will be new and important information that will make our story more complete. And, in all likelihood, alter the story I've told. As a researcher, I'm comfortable with the fact that at the moment in time I gathered my information, I used the best information available. And I tried to get it as close to right as I could.

With five decades since graduation, we can look back and more clearly see how our history-making class impacted the university. Institutional transformation is difficult, to put it mildly. But it is so important if we are to realize systems and organizations that support equity, diversity, and shared power and leadership. Sometimes the trailblazers and pioneers lose faith, give up, or, in the words of psychologist Tomi-Ann Roberts, are undermined "by a thousand cuts."[1] From my research, it seems to me that President Shannon wasn't always served well in his attempts at moving the university toward coeducation. The numerous committees he established to study the issue and eventually to begin planning for the arrival of women sometimes slow-walked the process, which hindered any timely progress being made. And women had grown weary. Words such as "fight" and "battle" were often used to describe UVA's coeducation path, and despite some saying that the better angels would have prevailed, and coeducation would have happened when it did without a court case, all indications are that this is not entirely true. As Kevin Mannix (Arts and Sciences, '71; Law, '74) stated fifty years later, "Yes, it would have happened. But not when it did and not like it did."

Among the many things that have changed since my classmates and I were at UVA, the women's studies major, established in 1989, is now the Department of Women, Gender, and Sexuality. Over the years, the university established various committees and task forces on the status of women and in 1999 formed a Women's Leadership Council. The Women's Center, opened in 1989 under the direction of Sharon Davie, has expanded and become involved in more issues supportive of women and all students.

In 2010, UVA named Teresa A. Sullivan as its first woman president, and after a brief pause to assist Michigan State University, her alma mater, during a leadership transition, she returned to UVA to become the George M. Kaufman Presidential Professor in Sociology. In 2017, Carla Williams was named UVA's first Black female director of athletics. She leads one of the most complex departments at the university, with responsibility for supporting the athletic and academic lives of hundreds of UVA students and overseeing one of the largest budgets at the university. Fundraising, negotiating vendor contracts, and, more recently, assisting student athletes as they navigate the relatively new world of NIL, allowing them to be financially compensated for their names, images, and likenesses, are all in her wheelhouse.

The UVA community has recognized the gaps in recognition for women, minorities, and others who contributed, often with great personal hardship, to the progress of the university. Plaques, part of a change agent initiative, have been, and will continue to be, erected honoring women, such as Teresa Sullivan and Virginia Scott. A group picture of the women who entered UVA in 1970 was taken at our fiftieth reunion, May 31, 2024, and was dedicated and hung that fall in the Edgar Shannon Library. The University Guides created a special tour that recognized women's contributions to the university, and there is a self-guided walking tour available as well.

Probably the most important improvement is the acknowledgment of the need to make the Grounds safer and more secure for the women in the UVA community. Lighting, call buttons, and better patrolling of buildings and outside areas, augmented by a busing system that runs 24/7, are all part of today's university.

The Honor Code still does not include sexual abuse and rape as honor violations, and this omission will continue to be debated as both men and women question how being honorable can exclude preying on and harming a fellow student. In 2022 changes were made to the Honor Code's fundamental practices, suggesting that what constitutes honorable behavior will continue to be part of future conversations.

On April 16, 2022, Ceci Cain was sworn in as UVA's student council

Women became part of the University Guides program. (1972 *Corks and Curls*)

president. In her remarks she stated, "We must redefine the philosophies that underpin the systems at play in the University and in our broader world." She continued, "To work for students when women are here, when Black people are here, when those of us who were never meant to come to UVA—let alone succeed here—are here."[2]

There is great promise in the women—and men—who are part of today's University of Virginia community. The memories we hold dear are secondary to the dreams we have for the future UVA.

Impact on Individuals

In researching and writing this book, I've had to sit in the discomfort of allowing that multiple, even opposing things can be true—sometimes all at the same time. The women in my class each had a unique experience, and sometimes these experiences were vastly different. Some of my classmates recounted tremendous hardships, even trauma that marred their UVA experience. For others, those four years were some of the best of their lives. When we arrived at UVA in 1970, the university was both progressing and resisting change; it was welcoming and at times hostile. Diane Kirchner Knetzger (Arts and Sciences, '74) recalls this time as "an era of exploration, experimentation and, for the most part, peaceful activism. People were waking up and realizing what was important to them. People were opening their hearts and minds to change. There was more acceptance and cooperation towards a common good."

Personally, I am so grateful for my time at UVA and how it shaped my life, and I also acknowledge the ways in which it has failed others. I met some of my best friends during those four years, had so many laughs, adventures, and fun. I met my husband, my love, and the father of my two daughters, but I also can still remember some really awful moments, where my sense of belonging, a fundamental human need, was in question. I am proud to be one of the first undergraduate women at UVA and of the strides that we made, and there are days when I am frustrated by the university's lack of progress. All of that can be true. And it was. And it is.

Older and Wiser

I, along with many of my fellow classmates, have suffered from a variety of ills—including arthritis, bad knees, and cancer. Some of these ailments are directly related to aging and are more of an inconvenience than anything else. Our bodies are weaker and our minds sometimes forgetful. Some of us are still actively engaged in our career, and others of us fill our days with gardening, reading, traveling, philanthropic work, and grandchildren. And when we wake in the middle of the night, as all older people do, we think back on the years gone by and ask ourselves, "Was it worth it?"

But unlike other groups of women our age, we are the women, 367 strong, who entered UVA as first-year students in 1970. We chose to become a member of UVA's community, studying in the Academical Village, walking the hallowed Grounds designed by a president who was so proud of UVA that it was one of three things he wanted spelled out on his gravestone: "Father of the University of Virginia."

We accepted the invitation to enter UVA for a variety of reasons: financial, academic, to prove the naysayers who said we wouldn't "cut it" wrong, and, for some, to be part of history. One classmate, who was interested in attending an Ivy League college, changed her mind because, as she said, the chance to be in the first class of women was too good to pass up.

That doesn't mean that it was the right decision for all of us. Some left during our first year, and others didn't return for our second. The reasons according to Gibbs were varied, but it's fair to say that some didn't want to navigate the intersection of Old U and New U. Dean Ern, at ninety, responded emphatically when I asked if more women left before graduation than typical attrition. "Yes," he stated firmly into the phone. "Why wouldn't you? Many were ignored socially." He went on to add that it could have been much easier to get the full coeducational experience somewhere else.

James Roebuck, UVA's first African American student council president, spoke to the anti-coeducation sentiment at UVA. "I honestly believe there were men at UVA in 1970 who would have been happy to admit Black men to UVA, but did not want to admit women," he said. "They wanted to keep it a men's university."[3]

Those of us who spent all of our undergraduate years at UVA will never know if it would have been easier elsewhere, but it would have likely been less fraught than navigating the early tension caused by our presence on Grounds.

Like many of my classmates, I had no idea what to expect when I arrived at UVA. Our mere presence was a radical shift in the university's culture. Some of us had limited knowledge of UVA's coeducation journey, and others didn't think much about it. Some of us acknowledged our first year wasn't easy. But not much in life is. Some suggest that no college experience would likely be without some difficulties, given that no matter what college you attend you are still experiencing the first flush of independence and all the challenges that entails.

There were some who felt the pressure of representing not only ourselves, but all of our female classmates. Suzanne Keller, who in 1968 was appointed the first female professor at Princeton, said in *"Keep the Damned Women Out,"* "To be the first of anything is not easy. You can't make a mistake; you're on display all the time. Your failings become attributed not to you but to all women."[4]

Years later, many of my classmates describe a college journey that helped them gain confidence—in themselves and their ability to navigate hard times, to compete, and to excel in life. Those women who wrote of "job disappointments," or "finding themselves in an unhappy marriage," or receiving an unexpected health diagnosis suggest that they were better prepared for the curve balls life threw at them because of their time at UVA.

Betty Shotton (Arts and Sciences, '74) described in a 2011 article in *Virginia Magazine* how her four years at UVA equipped her for a career path often dominated by men. She wrote that the challenges she encountered "proved to be invaluable for me as I continued on a pioneering path for women in business and leadership throughout my career. I have been the fortunate beneficiary of many valuable lessons that only this specific moment in history could offer me."[5]

Claudia Russell (Architecture, '74) said, "Only in retrospect do I believe that we were essentially told that we could do anything. I am, as someone told me once, fearless. That person was an older relative who said that she wondered where that quality came from. At the time, I did not know. Now thinking back on it, perhaps we learned something about that quality at UVA."

Not surprisingly, some women indicated that they no longer thought much about their college days. It was, after all, long ago, and they have moved on. They have new worries and new journeys. Others lament that today's world apparently didn't take a clue from our struggles and challenges in the 1960s and 1970s. Brenda Weatherford Hagan (Nursing, '74), when interviewed in 2021, said, "Sadly, I feel we are losing some of the headway that had been made. I've participated in women's marches, fundraisers for women's health issues, Planned Parenthood events but see very few women in the 30–50 age range." She continued, "I have watched *Roe v. Wade* and other policy, opinion, public attitude changes with dismay. I fear we will lose women's right to choose through apathy." Unfortunately, Brenda's words proved prophetic.

Regardless of whether we continue to think about or reflect upon those youthful college years, they are part of us. They played a role in shaping us into the women we are today. And we helped shape the University of Virginia into what it is today. One classmate commented, "When you're in it, as it were, you just do what you have to do. You don't give the significance of what is happening, or how history will remember it, much thought."

Catherine (Katie) Kellett (Arts and Sciences, '74) remarked, "We created our own paths and ways of relating. I think it helped me to understand the fact that change is both inevitable and good, and to learn to embrace it. The value of diversity, the importance of listening and the need to trust are values that can never be overemphasized." Liz McLeod (Arts and Sciences, '74) said, "It is clear that many people are afraid of change. Our class demonstrated that change can strengthen us."

Kathleen McGinn (Arts and Sciences, '74) reflected on our role in UVA's progress, "Women in the first class started the transformative process that has resulted in the UVA of today, a preeminent academic institution. The mere presence of female students altered the landscape of the university and necessarily broadened the horizons. It became much more like the real world with its diversity of interests and problems. The admission of women served as the catalyst for enormous change."

Sisterhood Is Powerful

Sociologists, anthropologists, and members of the medical profession have described the beneficial role friends and family play in happiness and longevity. The women who entered UVA in 1970 are now living into a new season of life, and their friends often become their dominant support system. Many of my classmates found lifelong friends at UVA. Barbara Wilkinson (Arts and Sciences, '74), who never thought she would be able to attend UVA because of her family's limited means, reflected, "I owe much to the University, but the enduring friendships that were formed in those four years—priceless."

In contrast, some women reported leaving UVA without knowing a lot of women or having long-term friendships. Some made more male friends than female. Some lamented that they never found the friendships that their mothers or sisters found after attending schools with more balanced enrollments. Some assumed that because there were so few of us, we would band together and be a force, but they didn't encounter the comradery that they had expected. We held our own, but for some during those first few years, it was as individuals.

One classmate suggested that the suite-style living situations might have contributed to some of the difficulty in meeting other women. She offered that living on a hall, like many of the men did at the time in the old dorms, might have created greater opportunity for interaction with more women. Or possibly bringing sororities in earlier during our tenure at UVA may have helped in building female friendships. Some classmates believe that the sheer numbers alone account for why some of us left with few female friends.

The Good Old Days

Many of my classmates speak of their four years at UVA as idyllic. "It was a carefree time, even if I didn't know it then," one woman responded. "I met so many interesting people and my thinking was stretched, and my horizons expanded." Another said, "When I have to think of something pleasant, for example when I'm in the dentist's chair, I close my eyes and I see myself at eighteen, sitting on the Lawn with the Rotunda in front of me, framed by blue skies and puffy white clouds and I couldn't be in a happier place."

When I think about my four years at UVA, I can hear laughter. My friends and I had so much fun, often entertaining ourselves, sometimes entertaining others. It's a part of my UVA experience that I will always cherish.

Against the backdrop of turbulent times, we were hopeful. One classmate said she was recently listening to music from the 1960s and 1970s, and despite the Vietnam War and the Nixon years of lies and deceit, she remembered being filled with the sense of possibility. Being young, like the Tams sang, provided us a long runway to fulfilling our dreams.

We Emerged Prepared

Many of my classmates talked about how, after their four years at UVA, they felt prepared for just about anything. They saw this as a positive result of navigating the sometimes treacherous path of the first years of coeducation. Classmates speak of the confidence they gained by being a member of our pioneering class of women. One classmate reported, "I got kicked around in my career, like a lot of people, but I survived. I think I learned how because of my experiences at UVA." Women who found themselves in male-dominated careers believed they were more comfortable because of their years at a male-dominated university. Barbara Savage (Arts and Sciences, '74) said:

> One of the things that ironically was really important to me at UVA was that it completely demystified the notion of white male superiority, in every way. After UVA, I went to law school and I worked on Capitol Hill, which is about as white male as you can get. And what I mean when I say demystify— I really mean that when you walk into that space, you're not afraid of that, you're not intimidated by it, you know who you're dealing with, you know how to deal with it. So that's one of the ironic takeaways for me of being in an institution that was so predominantly white, male, and where I made really great relationships and have really great friends now. But in any event that was a training ground for me for the professional world that many of us went into.

Finding our voice, no easy thing for any woman, may have happened sooner rather than later for some of us. For many, the unique environment we encountered at UVA helped us gain confidence and feel comfortable in situations where we were greatly outnumbered by men, a situation that would be paralleled for many of us when we began and advanced in our careers. Alarie Tennille (Arts and Sciences, '74) reported that she was not surprised by the pay inequality she faced in her first job, but she was angered by it. She believes her years at UVA served to give her the fortitude to work against this practice.

Deborah (Debby) Denno (Arts and Sciences, '74), the Arthur A. McGivney Professor of Law and founding director of the Neuroscience and Law Center at Fordham Law School, reflected on her career path: "I was amazed that one of my suitemates knew when we arrived that she would be going to law school. I had no clue what I wanted to do. My parents were very traditional. Although they both had college degrees, and my father had a Ph.D., their plans were that college would polish me and I would find a nice husband. Yet, UVA's intellectual expanse and vibrant community propelled my own plans. I pursued a Ph.D. at Penn and later a law degree there. It certainly wasn't a straight path to what I'm doing now, but it got me to where I am today, and I feel very fortunate for that."

Persevere

In 2022, President Joe Biden nominated Judge Ketanji Brown Jackson to become the 116th associate justice of the United States Supreme Court (SCOTUS). Her confirmation hearing was infuriating and heartbreaking, to say the least. I am ashamed of the disrespect shown to the capable, brave, and experienced SCOTUS nominee by some members of the Congressional Judiciary Committee whose agendas were anything but determining her qualifications for the court. I was so moved by her grace in navigating a situation where she had so little control and endured such despicable behavior from predominantly power-wielding men. Judge Jackson told a story that illustrated her own freshman college experience. She recalled that she was trying to get her footing at a northeastern Ivy League college, far different than the high school she had attended in Miami, Florida. She was feeling overwhelmed and uncertain, which must have been written all over her as she traversed the Cambridge campus. And as she walked, a Black woman, a total stranger, approached her, looked her in the eyes, and said, "Persevere."[6]

Dean Ern purportedly looked for women who would persevere. He wanted the first class of women to be successful. In the *Gritty Women* podcast, Giovana de Oliveira said to Dean Ern, "A lot of women I interviewed said you told them later that you were looking for gritty women. What did you mean by that?" He responded, "Well, knowing it wasn't going to be a smooth pathway for the women coming in, I used the word gritty to say, 'Be tough, be tough. Put your spikes on and hold your ground.'" Ern took the job as dean of admissions, in part, he said, because he believed UVA would go coed soon after his appointment, and he wanted to be part of that transition. He also believed that the university would be better for it.[7] He continues to meet with women from our class, take pride in our accomplishments, and attend reunions. His one regret, he says half-jokingly, is that his daughters did not attend UVA.

Our Roads Ahead

My impetus for writing this book was quite simple. Like many of my classmates, I felt it was a story that needed to be told. As a member of the coeducating class at UVA, and someone also interested in understanding institutional change, I wanted to explore not only what it looked like but also what it *felt* like for the people whose mere presence at the time represented significant change. And certainly the fifty-year mark of our entry and, for most of us, our fiftieth graduation anniversary were significant. But it also was borne of current events of the mid-2020s—events that made it clear to me and many of my classmates that hard-won battles of equity and progress were in jeopardy.

Karen Skole (Arts and Sciences, '74) reflected on the parallels between the issues of the 1970s and today: "You don't think you have to be so vigilant, but you do. No one would have ever thought we would be seeing this level of divisiveness today." Events that felt eerily reminiscent to ones my classmates and I experienced. If "those who do not learn history are doomed to repeat it," then I will do my best to make sure, at the very least, our history is shared.

For the first-year women who entered UVA the late summer of 1970, the road ahead is now much shorter than the road behind us. Our energy is best spent, I think, in doing whatever we can to help create a world that is just and right for the current generation, and the one after that, and the one after that. A world where gender doesn't divide or restrict. We worry about our world where violence, climate change, and divisive politics threaten the future of our nation, and many of us are the new "gray panthers," marching, knocking on doors, and advocating for issues we believe in.

An apocryphal quote, often attributed to Winston Churchill goes, "If you're not a liberal when you're young, you have no heart, and if you're not a conservative when you're old, you have no brain." But psychologists suggest that when it comes to later-in-life beliefs, there are gender differences. Men often do become more conservative, but many women become more progressive and more involved in activism. Many of my classmates reported participating, as I did, in the Women's March of 2017 and other demonstrations that followed. One classmate said about the march, "I hadn't done anything like that since Vietnam." Carolyn Welch Brumbaugh (Arts and Sciences, '74), whose daughter was a student at Virginia Tech during the horrendous murders on their campus, said, "My daughter's life and mine changed in that instant." She continued, "I have become active in gun control organizations and will remain active until I die." Others spend time trying to slow, or even reverse, the effects of bad climate decisions, recognizing that our beautiful Earth is imperiled.

Our Alma Mater

When I asked my classmates about their current relationship with UVA, there was a variety of responses. Many continue to contribute to the university with their time, talents, and monetary resources. One classmate, anonymously, funds a scholarship for underrepresented students; several others support, advocate for, and help select scholarship recipients. One classmate and her husband funded extensive work on the gardens, and others support the Alumni Association, the Virginia Athletics Foundation, and Maxine Platzer Lynn Women's Center. Many travel regularly to UVA for sporting events and get-togethers with old classmates. Some have returned to the Charlottesville area to retire.

Other fellow alums describe a different relationship, one where they are still bothered by too much of the "Old U-ism" and the reports of continued challenges for Black, minority, and women students. Author and UVA alumnus Virginius Dabney wrote about UVA in 1981, "The country club of the south was now a nationally-ranked university."[8] Some still see the country club in today's university. Although women comprise more than 50 percent of entering classes, a number consistent with U.S. colleges and universities, they lag behind in key administrative positions and tenured faculty. In 2020, Black students made up 7.2 percent of UVA's undergraduate enrollment in a state that, according to census data, is 19.9 percent Black. In 1970, the percentage of Black students was 1.3 percent, according to university records, with the state reporting 18.5 percent Black citizenry. That number almost doubled, to 3.4 percent, during our four years at UVA.[9] Despite inroads in enrollment and other actions to bring equity to UVA, including a commission on diversity, some see progress as far too slow.

Preserving Our History

The university has marked the anniversaries of our entry with various activities. In 1995, on the twenty-fifth anniversary of our arrival, a series of events was held, including a forum with John Lowe and alumnae entitled "U-Chicks, Road Trips and the Arrival of Jill Wahoo."[10] Another forum was held at the forty-year mark, and as mentioned earlier in the book, the Alumni Association marked the fiftieth-year anniversary with an all-day virtual summit, ReTold, and follow-up webinars and Zoom panels. Reunions have drawn a core of alumnae who plan and attend a recurring session for the women in our class, with Dean Ern as a featured guest. He still speaks highly of our class, and many, including men in our class, credit him with "selecting" a group of women who not only did well but excelled.

At the twenty-fifth reunion event Ern said of the first group of women, "They were absolutely superstars. When they arrived here they became a very real challenge to the male population scholastically and certainly in the leadership realm."[11]

Dale Miller Hill (Arts and Sciences, '74) videotaped some of the reunion discussions and other gatherings and donated tapes and files to the archives. Funding has been obtained to transcribe sessions and make the historical documents more accessible.

Alumnae who helped plan our fiftieth reunion in 2024 were intentional about ensuring that sessions and activities recognized the contributions of the women in our class. A subcommittee, working with representatives from the College of Arts and Sciences, the Alumni Association, and the UVA Library, worked on follow-up sessions to further shine a light on the cadre of women who coeducated the university. Work to create an archival repository of documents and memorabilia from class members was underway as this book went to press.

Others have brought their children and grandchildren to spend time in Charlottesville, walking the Grounds and sharing stories of their years at UVA. Many of us take pride in the fact that our own children attended the university, as did my older daughter, Alison. For me, no visit to the university is complete without slipping into the Chapel where I was married the day before graduation. Another classmate married in the Chapel the afternoon after our walk on the Lawn.

On my more recent visits to the Grounds, to research this book, attend basketball games, and share the university with my older grandchildren, I am struck by the consistently polite, helpful, and interested students I meet. Wyatt Andrews (Arts and Sciences, '74), who after retiring as a newscaster came back to Charlottesville and taught media classes, said to me, "Gail, just like us, the students today know that being at UVA, they are somewhere special. That has stayed the same all these years."

If we long for anything, it's probably to have one more chance to run down the Lawn in our bare feet or play our music too loud without worrying about what it would do to our hearing (we now know what it did). We wish for a perfect cloudless day with a light wind and nowhere we need to be, where we can sit under a tree and look at the mountains and dream big dreams. In the words of Thomas Jefferson, "Man has no nobler or more valuable possession than time." And I choose to believe he would include women in this sentiment, too.

The university, for all its frailties, has been a testament for us, the women who arrived young and hopeful in the late summer of 1970, of the vision that Thomas Jefferson expressed for the University of Virginia on April 3, 1826: "I am closing the last scene of life by fashioning and fostering an establishment for the instruction of those who are to come after us. I hope its influence on their virtue, freedom, fame and happiness will be salutary and permanent."

Here once more: The women affiliated with the class of 1974 on the steps of the Rotunda, gathered during their fiftieth reunion, May 31, 2024. (Courtesy of UVA Communications; photo by Kelly West)

EPILOGUE

Do the best you can until you know better. Then, when you know better, do better.
　　　　　—Maya Angelou

IN MARCH 2022, MY husband and I were back on Grounds for the second time in a month. I had been trying to get records of admissions and enrollments from the registrar, the admissions office, the Office of Institutional Research and Analytics, and the vice president of research. Dean Ern and his wife, Petie, who still live locally, were both incredibly helpful and interested in this book, and Dean Ern had been searching through his old records. The librarians in the Special Collections Library were gems, never flinching when I requested more files.

Without any official documentation or records, we had been keeping count of the women in my class from the *First Year Directory for the Class of 1974,* or "facebook," which I bought for $1 more than fifty years ago. By cross-referencing the women listed there with the most recent reunion list, I found many of my female classmates. Then, by cross-referencing this list with the commencement program lists, a tedious but surprisingly successful strategy, I deduced approximate graduate rates. While this is not the ideal way to conduct research, it was the best I could do under the circumstances.

Then, one morning, I headed to the archives where more than twenty unprocessed boxes from the storage facility in Ivy Stacks awaited me and my husband, my unpaid, uncomplaining research assistant. In one of the last boxes, I found what I was looking for—or the best information I had found to date—a typed tally, with a handwritten correction, that Dean Ern submitted to the State Council of Higher Education for Virginia (SCHEV) with enrollment numbers for the 1970 entering class. *Eureka!*

Later that day, I received an email from an assistant to the current dean of admissions. I had previously contacted her in hopes of locating old files. On her way into work that day she saw a new plaque out front of Peabody Hall, the current admissions office, and sent me a picture. As chance would have it, we had seen it late the day before, right after its installation. It was spring break. Very few students were on Grounds, and it would probably be another week before many would notice. There were families walking the Grounds, including what looked to be high school students touring the campus, perhaps making decisions about their own college journeys.

The plaque reads, "ACLU Case Brings Full Coeducation to UVA." It shows the first page of the lawsuit, a photo of Virginia Scott, and another photo of women unpacking a car on move-in day in September 1969. The accompanying text provides a good summary of the lawsuit and includes the four complainants' names: Jo Anne Kirstein, Virginia Scott, Nancy Jaffe, and Nancy Anderson. As I read and reread the plaque, I asked myself who would stop to look at it, and if they would think much about its significance. Then, almost a year later, I was back at the archives, doing final fact-checking, and I stopped by the plaque again. Stuck to it with blue painter's tape was a small yellow sticky note with these words: "You are loved. Never forget that." It took a year, but I had my answer.

In the Alumni Association's magazine, published to mark the fiftieth anniversary of our arrival on Grounds, Richard Gard wrote an article called "Not without a Fight." In it, he spoke about the judge's ruling that made permanent the injunction allowing Virginia Scott to enter UVA in 1969. He said it cleared "the way for her to earn her undergraduate degree in 1973, a full year's bragging rights ahead of the women of the Class of 1974, celebrated as the first wave of College coeducation."

For the record and accuracy, at least four remarkable women who entered in September 1970 graduated a full year early in May 1973. Another graduated in August, and a handful finished in December 1973, technically graduating in January 1974. I think, too, it's important to clarify that coeducation wasn't a competition, it wasn't about winning, and it wasn't a race with "bragging rights." To make it one diminishes the accomplishments of all the women who, on this unique and important journey, persevered, and all wore "the honors of Honor."

The Question Remains

The $64,000 question, as they say, remains unanswered. What took UVA so long to admit women in numbers that mattered? Numbers that made a true difference in the makeup of the student body. It is a question that can never be answered, at least not fully or satisfactorily. Some historians say the answer is that UVA was never designed to be coed, and therefore the movement to include women was anathema to the founder's intent and fraught with conflict at every turn. Others state that it appears UVA evolved very quickly into an elite enclave of and for "Virginia Gentlemen," rich with the traditions and accoutrements of landed gentry. Still others believe that when UVA established itself as a "public" Ivy and disavowed "state-Uism," being all male was one other indicator of UVA's superiority.

Barry Parkhill (Education, '73) said the question of why it took so long to admit undergraduate women comes up often when he is talking with someone new to the university community. In today's world it seems inconceivable that a state university, supported by taxpayer dollars, would have ever excluded women. On the *Gritty Women* podcast, Giovana de Oliveira interviewed Anne Coughlin, the Lewis F. Powell, Jr., Professor of Law at UVA, who noted, "What's really striking when you look at the timeline, is how late UVA was. State universities in other southern states made the move to integrate *way* before we did, not just by a decade, but by decades."[1]

Men who were party to the transformation at UVA—among them, Shannon, Ern, Casteen, Lowe, Bagby, Mannix—were and are the first to acknowledge the benefit of coeducation. In her book about coeducation, Nancy Weiss Malkiel says that of the late adopting Ivies she studied, the change was a result of the work of men. This is true; however, context is important. Women did not have the power, position, or authority to enact changes in policies and practices. I would suggest that men may have done the initial work, but the heavy lifting was done by women.

Despite some foot dragging and unhappiness with the coeducation plan, every man I spoke to about this book saw coeducation as a good thing. When George Allen (Arts and Sciences, '74; Law, '77) was deciding which school he wanted to attend his second year, he said, "I was considering transferring to the University of Tennessee, the University of North Carolina at Chapel Hill, North Carolina State, Duke, and others. I wouldn't have bothered to take time to visit the University of Virginia if it wasn't coed."

As one of the women who lived through the experience of breaking the gender barrier, I think the reason UVA took so long to coeducate is this—pure and simple gender discrimination. By excluding women from admission to the College of Arts and Sciences, half of the people who would be vying for the top grades, honors, scholarships, and, later, jobs were eliminated. This answer, of course, has other complexities and may seem too simple, but it is, I believe, still true.

Wayne Cozart, a long-time administrator and UVA historian, said the timing for the first class of women was actually ideal because of the intersection of coeducation with other factors—both at the university and within society. He suggested that the May Day Strike, UVA's plan for growth, the legislation around Title IX, and the *Roe v. Wade* decision all created a nearly perfect environment for change. He suggested that UVA, in effect, became a new university.

Bill Keene (Arts and Sciences, '71) is a retired research professor in the Department of Environmental Science. In a video celebrating the fiftieth anniversary of that department, he addressed entering the program with the first undergraduate class in 1970. "It was a pretty dynamic time back then," he said. "The Vietnam War was raging, the first women's class entered at the same time, and the university was really in a state of flux."

Jan Gaylor Owen, in her doctoral dissertation on the Shannon years, states that during this period "a new University of Virginia was coming into being."[2]

Others recognized the changes to the University.

Coming full circle, Liz McLeod at the Women's March in Washington, D.C., January 21, 2017. (Courtesy of Liz McLeod)

Virginius Dabney said, "The decades of the sixties and the early years of the seventies witnessed significant changes in the size and makeup of the university's student body, and this, in turn, brought drastic revision of some time-honored attitudes and tradition, and customs. The enrollment of hundreds of [Black students] and thousands of women in the seventies could not fail to bring far-reaching breaks with the past." Dabney continued, "Faculty academic standards and intellectual level sharply upgraded and the students 'manifested a greatly augmented concern for the less fortunate elements of society.'"[3]

As I reflect on women at the University of Virginia and the gains we made, I am also aware that we haven't come far enough. I have examined the genesis, history, and systems in place that foster institutional sexism and allow it to exist and sustain. As I write this, the Equal Rights Amendment (ERA) still has not been ratified and become law, and the Violence Against Women Act recently passed after a lapse caused by the U.S. Senate leadership's refusal to schedule a hearing. Reproductive rights, legally guaranteed for almost fifty years after the Supreme Court decision in *Roe v. Wade* in 1973, are no longer afforded women when the Supreme Court ruled on June 24, 2022, in *Dobbs v. Jackson Women's Health Organization* that the Constitution does not confer the right to abortion. The 2020 Democratic presidential primaries raised the question, again, of whether a woman could be elected president. Some believe that a man was nominated, in part, because it was a "safer" option, ensuring a better chance of Democrats winning back the highest office.

Like millions of other women, I was profoundly moved by the testimony of Dr. Christine Blasey Ford during the hearings for Judge Kavanaugh's appointment to the Supreme Court in 2018. I watched the hearings, with a million emotions—despair, sadness, and anger among them. I found myself with tears in my eyes and a sense of helplessness at the lack of compassion and understanding on the part of many elected officials. I was moved to rage at the then Senate Majority Leader's labeling of a group of women who congregated in the Capitol, attempting to have their voices heard, as a "mob." That group included my younger daughter, an accomplished writer and author of scores of books, who graduated from a high school in the senator's hometown.

For many, Judge Kavanaugh's appointment was one of many indignities suffered by women during the 2016 campaign and subsequent actions of the Trump administration. My daughter related to me an incident at a meeting of NOW she attended soon after Donald Trump was elected president, in which a woman who self-identified as a member of the first class of women at UVA explained how difficult it was for her to be a witness to all that was transpiring because it brought up traumatic memories of her college years.

Troubled Times for the University of Virginia

The University of Virginia and Charlottesville have had their share of controversy in the years since we were students. Ghosts of the "Old U" surface from time to time, reclaiming the traditions that some believe were important to making UVA UVA. The university is steeped in tradition, and that tradition included practices and policies that were antithetical to diversity and inclusiveness. Indeed, the exclusiveness of UVA was often considered a positive feature, making admission even more coveted. At times there was a sense of superiority, garnered by social and academic exclusivity, all of which shaped sentiments about coeducation in the 1960s. Given that tension, then and now, it's important that the challenges around diversity, both past and present, are examined.

The 2012 forced resignation of Teresa A. Sullivan, the university's first female president, and her reinstatement surfaced issues of gender politics at the highest level of the university administration.[4] In 2014, *Rolling Stone* published an article that featured an account of a rape on campus, and the subsequent fallout brought to light a college culture of binge drinking and predation, even as the facts described in the article were deemed fabricated and later retracted.[5] That same year a female student was abducted and murdered.

In 2015, three white Alcoholic Beverage Control officers assaulted and arrested Martese Johnson, a Black student and member of the Honor Committee, which put a spotlight on the racism many Black students face in Charlottesville. In 2019, the state of Virginia's deep history of racism resurfaced when the photos of Virginia elected officials in blackface made front-page news, evoking the 2002 sanctioning of two UVA fraternities for hosting parties where some members in attendance wore similar minstrel makeup.[6]

In recent years the university has found it challenging to persuade UVA crowds singing "The Good Old Song," UVA's "fight song," to drop the words "NOT GAY," a tradition that some say started in the 1970s. More recently, a new slur emerged about Virginia Tech, a UVA instate rival, deemed by some as a "lesser" school in academic and social status. There have been attempts to change to a different "fight song," but in the summer of 2019, President James E. Ryan, still in his first year, appealed to students' and fans' school pride and "better angels," with a professionally produced video stating all the reasons why singing these slurs is beneath members of the UVA community.[7] At a home basketball game several months after the release of the video, it was apparent that not everyone was onboard with Ryan's sentiments.

A struggle that continues to this day has to do with continuing to honor men, through statues and building names, who have a history of racism, sexism, anti-Semitism, and homophobia. In 2017, plans were made to remove the statue of Robert E. Lee, erected in 1924 in Lee Park, since renamed Emancipation Park, that commemorates the Lost Cause and celebrates the Confederacy. On August 11 of that year, a crowd of tiki-torch-wielding white supremacists descended on the city in protest for what they called the "Unite the Right" rally. What transpired was one of the most visible and horrifying incidents in recent history, resulting in the death of an innocent young woman and altering the lives and landscape of the Charlottesville and UVA community.

In his book *Confessions of a Free Speech Lawyer: Charlottesville and the Politics of Hate,* Rodney A. Smolla writes that "Charlottesville became the epicenter of the national debate over Confederate monuments." The Unite the Right rally held in Charlottesville, with a trip through the Grounds the night before, was organized by representatives from a number of white supremacy groups, among them two led by UVA graduates.[8] Barbara Savage (Arts and Sciences, '74) suggested to me that the events in Charlottesville in the summer of 2017 were a prelude to the January 6, 2021, insurrection at our nation's Capitol, one of the most shocking and disturbing events in my lifetime.

In each of these examples, to the credit of the university administration, faculty, and students, the situations have resulted in exploration of root causes, recognition of the challenges, and steps to advance remedies. UVA has been recognized for its efforts in addressing and celebrating diversity, such as recently being ranked as the seventh best college or university for LGBTQ students. In 2018, *Forbes* magazine ranked UVA among the nation's top employers, especially for women. In 2019, in recognition that university buildings were built by enslaved people, UVA broke ground for a Memorial to Enslaved Laborers on land adjacent to the Rotunda. The Memorial, now completed, is a visually stunning and powerful addition to the Grounds and is visited often by students, alumni, and community members. A multimillion-dollar donation to recruit and support first-generation college students was recently made by UVA alumni, and in January 2020 President Ryan announced a new initiative known as "inclusive excellence," which he stated is "a model that will advance the critical role of diversity and inclusion at UVA."[9]

I truly believe that a good education is a right, and a great education is a gift. And I was fortunate to be given that gift. In elementary school as well as junior and senior high I had caring, competent, and hard-working teachers who felt successful when their students learned and achieved. At UVA I had professors who challenged me to think deeply, to question, and to resist easy answers. They helped me find a career path that was stimulating and meaningful. It was at UVA that I discovered the power of a community whose members read, debated, and were thoughtful about and committed to making the world a better place. I've tried to live a life of purpose, fully aware that I have been given a lot and am truly privileged. Like my classmates, I have plans for this next chapter of life, plans that include being intentional about using my time on things that matter, that will make a difference.

In an afterword for what would be her final book, Madeleine Albright writes about resilience, "To me, resilience of spirit (far more than brilliance or intellect) is the essential ingredient of a full life. No matter how smart we are, we can allow sorrows and grievances to overwhelm us, or we can respond positively to setbacks—be they caused by our own misjudgments or forces beyond our control."[10]

She centered her reflections against "not only the pandemic but also from doubts about our willingness to pursue social justice, our power to make self-government succeed, and our capacity to prevent advanced technology from causing more harm than good." She continued, "Worldwide, we have undergone a period of trial that has changed us in ways not fully revealed."

Her final charge: "So let us buckle our boots, grab a cane if we need one, and march."

Yes, we've been changed in ways "not fully revealed." And the longer we live, the more we will change and be changed. As we did fifty-odd years ago, we will meet head-on the ever-evolving world in which we live—but now with even more experience, more knowledge, and more grit.

We did it before, and we'll do it again.

AFTERWORD

Like the author, I grew up in a small town outside a large city. LaGrange, Georgia, is about an hour south of Atlanta and offered me a lot growing up. My family loved sports and encouraged me to play. Fortunately, there was a recreation center down the street from my house, and I took full advantage. I played tennis, volleyball, softball, and basketball, and I swam. I even played football with the boys up until I went to high school!

Neither of my parents had gone to college, but they encouraged me to use my passion for sports as a pathway to a better life. I attended the University of Georgia on a basketball scholarship, then became an assistant coach after I graduated. I later earned my doctorate in education.

Like the women who entered the University of Virginia in 1970, I've grown accustomed to people underestimating me. I've had to face the antiquated stereotype that women aren't as good at sports as men, and even the belief that women aren't as good at leading as men. But if I had listened when people said, "You can't do that," or "You aren't good enough," I wouldn't be where I am today. Instead, I've bet on myself over and over again. I think that's one of the wonderful things that sports taught me—it's given me the confidence to compete. When you believe and have the confidence to compete, you can do anything.

In 2017, when I started as the athletic director (AD) at the University of Virginia, I became the first African American female in that role at any Power Five conference school. I was extremely honored and excited to become UVA's AD. It was a position that I had dreamt of and worked hard for. I knew I could do the job, and I knew I could do it well. Still, though, I had to fight to be considered. And then, when I settled in to my office in the McCue Center, the same recurring theme entered my mind as I longed for the calming familiarity of someone else who looked like me, someone I could lean on for advice, for support, or for reassurance.

In many ways, I relate to the women in these pages, the women who arrived on Grounds in 1970. I know what it means—and what it feels like—to be first, to blaze a trail in uncharted territory. The unknown is both thrilling and scary. The honor of being a pioneer brings both pressure and privilege.

In the years since I have been at UVA, we have faced many challenges and some devastating heartbreaks, but I am proud of the ways we've traversed these difficult times, together. And although there were no official athletic teams for the women who entered in 1970, the stories in this book suggest that the women in this pioneering class banded together and leaned on each other in both the good times and the bad times.

Something else I have learned about the University of Virginia community is that the students and alumni love this school. They are proud of their alma mater and are invested in its success. And although I am not a student or alumna, I am part of the UVA community, and I love this university, too.

From the moment I became a Cavalier, I had big dreams—and detailed plans—for UVA Athletics. I made it a goal to ensure that all student athletes have access to the tools and resources they need to excel in the classroom, in their sport, and in life. That includes opportunities for growth as leaders, career development, championship-level facilities, excellence in athletic performance, skills to navigate and thrive during adversity, and increased access and opportunities for marginalized athletes, coaches, and administrators. We have so much to be proud of, and still much to do.

As I reflect on the journeys of this class of women who coeducated UVA, as well as my own journey, I am aware that it is an awesome position to be in, to forge a path for others to follow. I know, too, the responsibility that comes with being first. This responsibility, I believe, is to look around to see who else you can bring along, who else you can mentor, motivate, encourage, educate, and equip. As my own children are well aware, "To whom much is given, much is required." That is what I aim to do every day in my work at UVA.

As Gail wrote in the dedication, we all stand on the shoulders of those who came before us. And, without a doubt, some of the shoulders on which I stand belong to the women who entered UVA in the late summer of 1970. I am forever grateful to them for their perseverance and grit. They had the nerve to defy the odds, and I love that. May they continue to lead and innovate in this next chapter of their lives.

Carla Williams
Athletic Director
University of Virginia

ACKNOWLEDGMENTS

The story of researching and writing this book could be its own book. The takeaway, though, of the starts and stops, frustrations, and bumps in the road, is that I learned a lot. And I made some friends along the way. Not a bad trade-off.

I am so grateful to the many people who assisted me in bringing this book to life:

First and foremost, to my classmates, most named and some not, who shared their stories and gave me permission to include them.

Ginger, who showed enormous courage and who paved the way.

Former and current administrators, professors, students, and staff members at UVA, especially those at the Shannon Library, the Law Library, and the archives at Small Special Collections, including but not limited to Holly, Lauren, Anne, Penny, Stephanie, Randi, and John.

The team at the University of Virginia Press, especially Suzanne, who as acting director supported this project when it needed a boost: Mark, Boyd, Eric, Mary Kate, Ellen, Cecilia, Clayton, Jane, Rebecca, and more—my sincere appreciation.

Helpmates at the Alumni Association, especially Jess, Liz, Savannah, and Lily, whose support and creativity helped me reach more of my classmates.

Terry and Carla, two glass-ceiling-breakers, who added their voices to our story, as only those with their lived experiences could.

Dickie, Patty, Barry, Susan, Scott, and Wyatt, who stepped in at critical junctures, and whose time and attention devoted to the research process and the manuscript development were immeasurably helpful.

Alice, Brenda, Debby, and Stephanie—my beloved "Ypsi Chicks."

Annette, Karen, Lynn, and Scott—my dearest of friends who shored me up when I needed it most, and to Dean and Tom, my eternal advocates and mentors.

Paul, Linda, Lori, Tom, Robin, and Terri—my first family and forever champions. And to my parents, who I know would be proud.

Liz, Margaret, and Patty, who, during our monthly book club meetings, unfailingly asked me about the book's progress, cheering me on.

Alison, my keen-eyed and whip-smart daughter, who provided help, encouragement, and Trader Joe's treats along the way, and my son-in-law Dan, a proud Virginian.

Lisa, editor, researcher, and project manager extraordinaire, who, with the kindness only a daughter can give, lent her professional skills, knowledge, and expertise throughout the process.

Larry, steady and steadfast, by my side throughout. I fell in love with him at eighteen, and my love only grows.

And, maybe most importantly, my three grandchildren—Abigail, Andy, and Jackson—who gave me the motivation and determination to tell the story of the evolution of my alma mater, a place that for too long used tradition as a smokescreen for inequitable practices.

This book was written with love and respect for education, for a school, for progress, for my classmates, for my friends, and for my family—and it's with love and respect that I now offer it to you.

Let us learn from the past.

CHRONOLOGY

1967	April–June	President Shannon appoints committee to study need for women at UVA
		Vietnam War expands with over 500,000 U.S. troops in southeast Asia
1968	April–June	Civil rights leader Martin Luther King Jr. assassinated, April 4, 1968, followed by urban unrest
	July–September	Presidential candidate Robert F. Kennedy assassinated, June 5, 1968
	October–December	Woody Report recommends admission of women at UVA
		Richard Nixon wins presidency over Hubert Humphrey, November 5, 1968
		Deadliest year in Vietnam with 16,899 fatalities
1969	January–March	Hereford committee recommends limited admission of women over ten years
		UVA Coat and Tie Rebellion, February 16, 1969, demands more minority and women admissions
	April–June	John C. Lowe (Law, '67), sues UVA in federal court in Richmond, May 29, 1969, to force the admission of women
	July–September	Apollo Moon Landing, July 16, 1969
		Woodstock Music and Art Fair, August 15–18, 1969
		Federal judge orders UVA to allow Virginia Scott to enroll in September 1969

1969	October–December	News of My Lai Massacre reaches American public
		BOV approves two-year phase-in plan for women, October 1969, with unrestricted coeducation in fall 1972
		Second deadliest year in Vietnam, with 11,780 U.S. fatalities
		First military draft lottery, December 1, 1969; UVA men to be inducted upon graduation
1970	January–March	National Environmental Policy Act (NEPA)
	April–June	First Earth Day, April 22, 1970
		U.S. invades Cambodia, widening Vietnam War
		Kent State students killed, May 4, 1970–May Day demonstrations at colleges across the U.S.
	July–September	First class of 367 undergraduate women enter College of Arts and Sciences
	October–December	Vietnam War divides country, 55,000 U.S. casualties by end of 1970
1971	January–March	UVA admissions applications soar
	April–June	Military draft ends college deferment for men with low lottery numbers
	July–September	Pentagon Papers released showing military deceived Congress and the public regarding progress of the Vietnam War
		Congress passes 26th Amendment, July 1, 1971, giving eighteen-year-olds the right to vote
1972	January–March	Shirley Chisholm, first woman and first Black person to announce run for president, January 25, 1972
		Equal Rights Amendment to the Constitution passed, March 22, 1972
	April–June	Watergate burglars arrested breaking into the Democratic National Headquarters, June 17, 1972
		Supreme Court confirmed the right of unmarried women to use birth control pill
	July–September	Title IX—prohibits discrimination in education/activities based on gender

1973	January–March	Supreme Court *Roe v. Wade* landmark case regarding abortion rights
		Military draft ends
		U.S. military leaves Vietnam
	April–June	Nixon fires White House Counsel John Dean
		Attorney General John Mitchell resigns
	July–September	Alexander Butterfield tells Watergate Committee of Nixon tapes
1974	April–June	First class of undergraduate women graduate from UVA, May 19, 1974
	July–September	Richard Nixon resigns presidency under prospect of impeachment, August 8, 1974
1975	July	Federal Title IX regulations for intercollegiate athletics passed by Congress

NOTES

Prologue

1. Willis, "Recurring Final Exam Dream?"
2. Cappetta, "What I Would Tell My 18-Year-Old Self."
3. Tough, *Years That Matter Most*, 11.
4. ReTold, webinar held on October 10, 2020, coordinated by the University Alumni Association in collaboration with the UVA Maxine Platzer Lynn Women's Center.
5. Richie D. Watson, "The Virginia Gentleman." *Encyclopedia Virginia*, https://encyclopediavirginia.org/entries/virginia-gentleman-the/.
6. Ern, Report to the State Council of Higher Education for Virginia; "UVA Lingo."
7. Powers, *Education of an Idealist*, xii.
8. Mayer, "Study of the Attitudes"; Robertson, "Modest Pioneers."
9. Ern, Report to the State Council of Higher Education for Virginia.
10. WHO COVID-19 Dashboard, World Health Organization, https://data.who.int/dashboards/covid19/cases?n=c; COVID Data Tracker, Centers for Disease Control and Prevention, https://covid.cdc.gov/covid-data-tracker/#datatracker-home.
11. Mather, "Suspect Arrested in Shooting Deaths of 3 UVA Football Players."
12. Apprey and Poe, *Key to the Door*, ix.
13. Grimwood, "By God, I Think They're Here to Stay."
14. Elmer O. Jaffe, quoted in Grimwood, "By God, I Think They're Here to Stay."

1. Changing Times

1. Michel, *Struggle for a Better South*.
2. Dylan, "The Times They Are a-Changin'."
3. Miller, "It Was about Time," 48.
4. John M. Cunningham, "Phyllis Schlafly: American Writer and Political Activist," *Encyclopedia Britannica*, updated June 28, 2024, https://www.britannica.com/biography/Phyllis-Schlafly.
5. Phyllis Schlafly, "Open Letter to VMI Alumni," June 11, 1996, Eagle Forum, https://eagleforum.org/column/1996/july96/7-11-96.html. The letter is reprinted in Brodie, *Breaking Out*, 59.

{187}

6. Perkins, *Yale Needs Women*.
7. Perkins, *Yale Needs Women*, 17.
8. Malkiel, *"Keep the Damned Women Out,"* 66.
9. Malkiel, *"Keep the Damned Women Out."*
10. Yovanovitch, *Lessons from the Edge*, 26.
11. Solomon, *In the Company of Educated Women*, 203.
12. *New York Times*, April 13, 1969, quoted in Perkins, *Yale Needs Women*, 29.
13. Perkins, *Yale Needs Women*.
14. "Admission of Women to the College of Arts and Sciences," Board of Visitors Minutes, February 15, 1969, https://xtf.lib.virginia.edu/xtf/view?docId=2006_01/uvaGenText/tei/bov_1969-02-15.xml;chunk.id=d25;toc.depth=1;toc.id=d25;brand=default.
15. Levine, "Profound Need for Our Traditions."
16. Dabney, *Mr. Jefferson's University*, 495.
17. Brodie, *Breaking Out*, 22.

2. UVA's Journey to Coeducation

1. Ihle, "Women's Admission to the University of Virginia," 182.
2. Ihle, "Women's Admission to the University of Virginia," 186.
3. Ihle, "Women's Admission to the University of Virginia," 184.
4. Ihle, "Women's Admission to the University of Virginia," 184.
5. Leffler, "Mr. Jefferson's University," 82.
6. Ihle, "Women's Admission to the University of Virginia," 186.
7. Ihle, "Women's Admission to the University of Virginia."
8. Leffler, "Mr. Jefferson's University," 95.
9. Committee on the Future of the University, Minutes, 1965–68.
10. Committee on the Future of the University, Minutes, 1965–68.
11. Salem, "Strong Hands on the Helm," 14.
12. Board of Visitors, Minutes, April 8, 1967, https://xtf.lib.virginia.edu/xtf/view?docId=bov/1960/bov_1967-04-08.xml;chunk.id=d20;toc.depth=1;toc.id=;brand=default.
13. Ihle, "Women's Admission to the University of Virginia."
14. Edgar F. Shannon to Lewis H. Hammond, May 26, 1967, Shannon Papers.
15. C. Venable Minor to Edgar F. Shannon, June 22, 1967, Shannon Papers.
16. Woody Committee, "Report."
17. The letters that follow written by T. Braxton Woody, Edgar Finley Shannon, James H. Croushore, and Albert R. Klein are contained in the Papers of the President.
18. "Albert H. Klein," UMW Theatre, University of Mary Washington, https://cas.umw.edu/theatre/department-of-theatre-and-dance/online-tour/klein-theatre/.
19. Woody Committee, "Report."
20. Alumni letters on admitting women to UVA are found in Committee on the Future of the University, Papers, 1965–68.
21. Peril, *College Girls*, 291.
22. Annette Gibbs, Oral History, 1991, 12.
23. Woody Committee, "Report."
24. Coeducation Committee of the Martin Luther King, Jr. Chapter of the Virginia Council on Human Relations to Edgar F. Shannon, Shannon Papers.

25. Ihle, "Women's Admission to the University of Virginia."
26. Woody Committee, "Report."
27. Ihle, "Women's Admission to the University of Virginia," 185–86.
28. Kirstein v. Rector and Visitors of Univ. of Virginia, 309 F. Supp. 184 (E.D. Va. 1970), https://law.justia.com/cases/federal/district-courts/FSupp/309/184/2096076/.
29. T. Braxton Woody to Thomas B. Gay, January 6, 1969, in Shannon Papers.
30. Curtis, "Imperfect Progress," 58.
31. Ihle, "Women's Admission to the University of Virginia."
32. Ihle, "Women's Admission to the University of Virginia."
33. Dean of Women's Final Report to Dean of Students B. F. D. Runk, April 1967, Gwathmey Papers.
34. Memo, Gwathmey's assistant to President Shannon, April 27, 1961, Gwathmey Papers.
35. Correspondence between Ralph Cherry and Dean Gwathmey, December 4, 1962, Gwathmey Papers.
36. Whitney, "Women and the University."
37. Mary Whitney, Annual Report of the Office of the Dean of Women, 1969, copy in Office of the Vice President for Student Affairs, Papers.
38. Philip J. Hirschkop, quoted in Gard, "Not without a Fight."
39. Mary Whitney obituary, Dignity Memorial, March 5, 2013, https://www.dignitymemorial.com/obituaries/hemet-ca/mary-whitney-10828642.
40. "Shannon Answers Coalition," *Cavalier Daily*, February 26, 1969; Newman, "New Portraits, Markers Honor Important Stories."
41. Dean Ern Papers, Office of the Vice President for Student Affairs, Papers.
42. David Salem, "Strong Hands on the Helm," Shannon Papers.
43. Gard, "Not without a Fight," 41.
44. B. F. D. Runk, Oral History, 46–47.
45. Kirstein v. Rector and Visitors of Univ. of Virginia; Kelly, "Case for Full Coeducation at UVA."
46. Gard, "Not without a Fight."
47. Committee on the Future of the University, Preliminary Report on the Feasibility and Means of the Admission of Women to the College 1969.
48. Kirstein v. Rector and Visitors of Univ. of Virginia; Kelly, "Case for Full Coeducation at UVA."
49. Mannix, "Breaking Barriers," Minority Report on the Admission of Women.
50. Kirstein v. Rector and Visitors of Univ. of Virginia.
51. *Charlottesville Daily Progress*, August 25, 1970.
52. Shannon, quoted in Salem, "Strong Hands on the Helm," 17.

3. The First Cadre of Women

1. "Grit," APA Dictionary of Psychology, American Psychological Association, https://dictionary.apa.org/grit.
2. Duckworth, *Grit*.
3. Brodie, *Breaking Out*, 97.
4. Meacham, *Thomas Jefferson*, 18.
5. 1970 orientation materials, author's personal artifacts.

6. "Feminine Attitudes," *Cavalier Daily*, April 25, 1970.
7. Mary Whitney to incoming students, March 23, 1970, author's personal artifacts.
8. Annette Gibbs, Oral History.

4. By God, I Think They're Here . . .

1. Ern, Report to the State Council of Higher Education for Virginia.
2. First Year Council of 1973, University of Virginia, *The First Year Directory of the Class of 1974*, 1970, author's personal artifacts.
3. Annette Gibbs, Oral History.
4. *Cavalier Daily*, May 14, 1969.
5. Alumni Survey Project.
6. Elzinga, "50,000 Students and Counting."
7. Gibbs, Oral History.
8. Whitney, Annual Report of the Office of the Dean of Women, 1969, copy in Office of the Vice President for Student Affairs, Papers.
9. H. S. Dabney letter, author's personal artifacts.
10. *Daily Progress* circular, September 14, 1970.
11. T. Braxton Woody, Oral History.
12. Couric, *Going There*, 245.
13. Dabney, *Mr. Jefferson's University*, 492.
14. "1982: The Rise and Fall of Easters."
15. Funkhouser, "Va. Gentlewomen Meet a Man's World."
16. Gibbs, Oral History, 1991.
17. Robertson, "Modest Pioneers."
18. Leffler, "Mr. Jefferson's University," 98.
19. Mary Ann Huey, "Our Evolving Narrative: Alumnae Reflections across Generations" (webinar), October 20, 2020.
20. Whitney, Annual Report of the Office of the Dean of Women, 1969, copy in Office of the Vice President for Student Affairs, Papers.
21. Gibbs, Oral History.

5. . . . To Stay

1. Ihle, "Women's Admission to the University of Virginia."
2. Institutional Research and Analytics, University of Virginia, "University Data," https://ira.virginia.edu/.
3. Annette Gibbs, Oral History, 1991.
4. Owen, "Shannon's University," 296.
5. Gibbs, Oral History.
6. Gibbs, Oral History.
7. Dabney, *Mr. Jefferson's University*, ch. 8.
8. Bromley, "Symposium Traces History of African-American Studies."
9. *Cavalier Daily*, February 10, 1972.
10. Gard, "Not without a Fight."

11. See Williams Papers.
12. Ellison, "Shadows on the Lawn."
13. Mary Whitney, memo to D. Alan Williams, October 1969, Williams Papers.
14. Mayer, "Study of the Attitudes."
15. Ihle, "Women's Admission to the University of Virginia."
16. Bellows, King, and Rathbone, "Women at the University of Virginia."
17. Gibbs, Oral History.
18. *Cavalier Daily*, March 5, 1969.
19. White, "'Accidental Athlete' Helped Lead the Way."
20. Undated photo in *Corks and Curls*.
21. Bluey, "Dobbs Decision Explained."
22. Gibbs, Oral History.
23. Counselors Committee on Human Sexuality, "Ounce of Prevention."
24. *Corks and Curls*, 1973.
25. Robertson, "Modest Pioneers," 122.
26. Bellows, King, and Rathbone, "Women at the University of Virginia."
27. UVA Maxine Platzer Lynn Women's Center, "Welcome and FAQ," https://womenscenter.virginia.edu/about/welcome-faq.
28. Owen, "Shannon's University."

6. Trailblazers and Pioneers

1. Schlechty, "On the Frontier of School Reform."
2. Kelly, "Case for Full Coeducation at UVA."
3. Gard, "Not without a Fight."
4. Dean Ern, handwritten notes, in Office of the Vice President for Student Affairs, Papers.
5. Carla Williams, presentation delivered at National Girls and Women in Sports Day and the Fiftieth Anniversary of Title IX, UVA, February 6, 2022.
6. Giovana de Oliveira, interview with Barbara M. G. Lynn, *Gritty Women* (podcast), 2021.
7. "Meet Barbara and Mike Lynn."
8. Dallas Association of Young Lawyers, "DAYL Judge Barbara Lynn Continuing the Conversation."
9. Faderewski, "Dallas Bar Announces Chief Judge Barbara M. G. Lynn."
10. Harold and Everson, *Accidental Athlete*.
11. "Rector and Visitors of the University of Virginia," 46–47.

7. The World We're Living Into

1. "Undermined by a Thousand Cuts."
2. Cecilia Cain, UVA student council president inauguration speech, April 16, 2022.
3. Newman, "Former Student Council President Reflects on 'May Days.'"
4. Keller, quoted in Malkiel, *"Keep the Damned Women Out,"* 229.
5. Shotton, "Simple Things Said It All."

6. Dwyer, "Ketanji Brown Jackson Shares the Message."
7. Giovana de Oliveira, interview with Dean Ernest Ern, *Gritty Women* (podcast).
8. Dabney, *Mr. Jefferson's University*, 467.
9. University of Virginia, Institutional Research and Analytics, "University Data," https://diversitydata.virginia.edu; U.S. Census Bureau, Race and Ethnicity, 2020, https://data.census.gov/profile/Virginia?g=040XX00US51#race-and-ethnicity; U.S. Census Bureau, Race of the Population of the United States, by States: 1970, https://www2.census.gov/library/publications/decennial/1970/pc-s1-supplementary-reports/pc-s1-11.pdf.
10. UVA Alumni Association, 25th anniversary brochure.
11. UVA Alumni Association, 25th anniversary brochure.

Epilogue

1. Giovana de Oliveira, interview with Anne Coughlin, *Gritty Women* (podcast).
2. Owen, "Shannon's University," 296.
3. Dabney, *Mr. Jefferson's University*, 467.
4. Rice, "Anatomy of a Campus Coup."
5. Quinlan, "Rolling Stone Story Had a Lasting Effect."
6. Argetsinger, "U-Va. Frats Cleared in Blackface Incident."
7. "Keep 'The Good Old Song' Good," *UVA Today*, September 3, 2019, https://news.virginia.edu/video/keep-good-old-song-good.
8. Smolla, *Confessions of a Free Speech Lawyer*.
9. Bromley, "Ryan and McDonald Introduce UVA's 'Inclusive Excellence' Framework."
10. Albright, afterword to *Hell and Other Destinations*.

BIBLIOGRAPHY

Archival Materials

The following materials are located in the Albert and Shirley Small Special Collections Library, University of Virginia.

Alumnae Survey Project. University of Virginia, 1996, Accession #RG-30/25/1.071.
Archives Reference File. University of Virginia, 1924–2010. Accession #RG-12/12/1.081.
Associate Dean of Students, University of Virginia. Papers, 1973–1983. Accession #RG-18/2/1.832.
Burnett, David, and Phyllis K. Leffler. "Politics and Ideology Underlying the Transition to Coeducation at the University of Virginia." 1998. Accession #RG-22/1/1.982.
Committee on the Future of the University (COFU). Minutes and Papers, 1965–68. Accession #RG-20/18/2.751
Dale Hill Papers, MSS 16583.
Dean of Women, University of Virginia. Papers, 1914–1969. Accession #RG-34/1/1.701.
Ern, Ernest H. Report to the State Council of Higher Education for Virginia (Ern Report), November 4, 1970. Document 11.4.70. Records of the Office of Institutional Assessment and Studies, ca. 1960–2001. Accession #RG-3/4/4.161.
"Graduating Exercises." University of Virginia, 1908.
Gwathmey, Roberta Hollingsworth. Papers, ca. 1947–1970. Accession #RG-12772.
Lawn Resident Survey Project. 1996. Accession #RG-25/3/1.971.
Office of Institutional Assessment and Studies, University of Virginia. Records, ca. 1960–ca. 2001. Accession #RG-3/4/4.161.
Office of the Vice President for Student Affairs, University of Virginia. Papers, 1969–2001. RG-18/2/1.031.
President, University of Virginia. Papers. Accession #RG-2/1/2.711, #RG-2/1/2.731, #RG-2/1/2.741.
Salem, David. "Strong Hands on the Helm." Copy in Shannon Papers, MSS 12706-d.
Shannon, Edgar Finley. Papers. MSS 12706-d.
Student Council Papers. University of Virginia, 1969–72. Accession #RG-23/2/4.752.
"University of Virginia: Women at the University of Virginia between 1920–1976." Office of President John T. Casteen III, 1998.

"The University of Virginia in the Decade of the Seventies." 1972 April. Accession #RG-20/18/1.771.
Whitney, Mary E. "Women and the University." In collaboration with Rebecca S. Wilburn. Unpublished manuscript, 1969. Revised and expanded, 2002. LD5678.W55.
Williams, D. Alan-Worthington. Office of University Communications Administrative Files, Accession #RG-2/7/1.141.
Woody Committee (University of Virginia Special University Committee on the Admission of Women to the College of Arts and Sciences of the University of Virginia at Charlottesville). T. Braxton Woody, chair. "Report of the Special University Committee on the Admission of Women to the College of Arts and Sciences of the University of Virginia at Charlottesville." 1968.

Primary and Secondary Sources

Adams, Natalie G., and James H. Adams. *Just Trying to Have School: The Struggle for Desegregation in Mississippi*. Oxford, MS: University Press of Mississippi, 2018.
Albright, Madeleine. Afterword to *Hell and Other Destinations: A 21st Century Memoir*. New York: HarperCollins, 2020.
Alumni Association, University of Virginia. 25th Anniversary Brochure. 1995.
Apprey, Maurice, and Shelli M. Poe, eds. *The Key to the Door: Experiences of Early African American Students at the University of Virginia*. Charlottesville: University of Virginia Press, 2014.
Argetsinger, Amy. "U-Va. Frats Cleared in Blackface Incident." *Washington Post*, December 3, 2002.
Bellows, Sierra, Carianne King, and Emma Rathbone. "Women at the University of Virginia." *Virginia Magazine*, Spring 2011.
Bluey, Rob. "The Dobbs Decision Explained." *Daily Signal*, June 24, 2022. https://www.dailysignal.com/2022/06/24/the-dobbs-decision-explained/.
Breaking and Making Tradition: An Exhibition in Special Collections. Alderman Library, University of Virginia, May 16–November 3, 2003.
Brodie, Laura Fairchild. *Breaking Out: VMI and the Coming of Women*. New York: Pantheon Books, 2000.
Bromley, Anne E. "Ryan and McDonald Introduce UVA's 'Inclusive Excellence' Framework." *UVA Today*, January 16, 2020. https://news.virginia.edu/content/video-ryan-and-mcdonald-introduce-uvas-inclusive-excellence-framework.
Bromley, Anne E. "Six Memorable Milestones for Women at UVA." November 15, 2017, https://news.virginia.edu/content/six-memorable-milestones-women-uva.
Bromley, Anne E. "Symposium Traces History of African-American Studies at the University." *UVA Today*, April 11, 2011. https://news.virginia.edu/content/symposium-traces-history-african-american-studies-university.
Bruni, Frank. *Where You Go Is Not Who You'll Be: An Antidote to the College Admissions Mania*. New York: Grand Central, 2016.
Cappetta, Kristina. "What I Would Tell My 18-Year-Old Self." *HuffPost*, October 4, 2016. https://www.huffpost.com/entry/what-i-would-tell-my-18-year-old-self_b_12331514.

Counselors Committee on Human Sexuality, University of Virginia. "An Ounce of Prevention: Human Sexuality and the Student." Rev. ed., Student Council, University of Virginia, Charlottesville, 1973.
Couric, Katie. *Going There*. New York: Little, Brown, 2021.
Curtis, Tami Lynn. "Imperfect Progress: Coeducation at the University of Virginia." MA thesis, University of Virginia, 1987. doi.org/10.18130/V3J33F.
Dabney, Virginius. *Mr. Jefferson's University: A History*. Charlottesville: University Press of Virginia, 1981.
Dallas Association of Young Lawyers. "DAYL Judge Barbara Lynn Continuing the Conversation." September 5, 2018, YouTube. https://www.youtube.com/watch?v=3v2HtOaaK1c.
de Oliveira, Giovana. *Gritty Women* (podcast). Virginia Audio Collective, 2021. https://open.spotify.com/show/1io8wEQTvVYcapoCeyVCz2.
Duckworth, Angela. *Grit: The Power of Passion and Perseverance*. New York: Scribner, 2016.
Dwyer, Dialynn. "Ketanji Brown Jackson Shares the Message She Received from a Stranger in Harvard Yard." *Boston Globe*, March 24, 2022. https://www.boston.com/news/politics/2022/03/24/ketanji-brown-jackson-harvard-yard-persevere/.
Dylan, Bob. "The Times They Are a-Changin'." 1963. Bob Dylan website. https://www.bobdylan.com/.
Ellison, Sarah. "Shadows on the Lawn." *Vanity Fair*, October 2015. https://archive.vanityfair.com/article/2015/10/shadows-on-the-lawn.
Elzinga, Kenneth. "50,000 Students and Counting, Kenneth Elzinga—54 Years of Teaching at UVA." Interview with Teresa Sullivan, 2021. YouTube. https://www.youtube.com/watch?v=ws_aqF5_G6c.
Faderewski, Adam. "Dallas Bar Announces Chief Judge Barbara M. G. Lynn as Inaugural DBA Jurist of the Year." State Bar of Texas, Texas Bar Blog, August 31, 2021. http://blog.texasbar.com/2021/08/articles/news.
Friedan, Betty. *The Feminine Mystique*. New York: W. W. Norton, 1963.
Funkhouser, Laura. "Va. Gentlewomen Meet a Man's World." *Cavalier Daily*, October 26, 1970.
Gard, Richard. "Not without a Fight: How UVA Granted Women Full Admission Sooner Rather than Basically Never." *Virginia Magazine*, Fall 2020. https://uvamagazine.org/articles/uva_admission_women_legal_fight.
Germain, Lauren J. *Campus Sexual Assault: College Women Respond*. Baltimore: Johns Hopkins University Press, 2016.
Grimwood, Steve. "By God, I Think They're Here to Stay." *Cavalier Daily*, September 14, 1970.
Harold, Claudrena, and Kevin Jerome Everson. *Accidental Athlete*. Short film, Virginia Film Festival, November 4, 2022.
Hitchcock, Susan Tyler. *The University of Virginia: A Pictorial History*. Charlottesville: University Press of Virginia, 1999.
Ihle, Elizabeth L. "Women's Admission to the University of Virginia: Tradition Transformed." In *Going Coed: Women's Experiences in Formerly Men's Colleges and Universities, 1950–2000*, edited by Leslie Miller-Bernal and Susan L. Poulson, 181–97. Nashville, TN: Vanderbilt University Press, 2004.
Kelly, Jane. "The Case for Full Coeducation at UVA Turned on a Late-Night Phone Call." *UVA*

Today, September 28, 2017. https://news.virginia.edu/content/case-full-coeducation-uva-turned-late-night-phone-call.

Leffler, Phyllis. "Mr. Jefferson's University: Women in the Village!" *Virginia Magazine of History and Biography* 115, no. 1 (January 1, 2007): 56–107.

Levine, Saul. "A Profound Need for Our Traditions." *Psychology Today*, February 28, 2017.

Malkiel, Nancy Weiss. *"Keep the Damned Women Out": The Struggle for Coeducation*. Princeton, NJ: Princeton University Press, 2016.

Manne, Kate. *Entitled: How Male Privilege Hurts Women*. New York: Random House, 2020.

Mannix, Kevin L. "Breaking Barriers." Minority Report on the Admission of Women, September 19, 1969. Kevin L. Mannix website, https://www.kevinmannix.com/breaking-barriers.

Mather, Mike. "Suspect Arrested in Shooting Deaths of 3 UVA Football Players; 2 Others Wounded." *UVA Today*, November 14, 2022. https://news.virginia.edu/content/suspect-arrested-shooting-deaths-3-uva-football-players-2-others-wounded.

MayDay: An Exhibition in Special Collections. Alderman Library, University of Virginia, 2021.

Mayer, Evelyn Ann. "Study of the Attitudes of a Sample of the Initial Class of First-Year Women Admitted to Resident Living at the University of Virginia." Ph.D. diss., University of Virginia, 1971.

Meacham, Jon. *Thomas Jefferson: The Art of Power*. New York: Random House, 2012.

"Meet Barbara and Mike Lynn, Dallas' Legal Power Couple." *Dallas Morning News*, April 26, 2014.

"Meet Dr. Dickie McMullan." YouTube. https://www.youtube.com/watch?v=KLBkCvRG4cs.

Michel, Gregg L. *Struggle for a Better South: The Southern Student Organizing Committee, 1964–1969*. New York: Palgrave Macmillan, 2004.

Miller, Ed. "It Was about Time." *Virginia Magazine*, Fall 2020.

Miller-Bernal, Leslie. "Coeducation: An Uneven Progression." In *Going Coed: Women's Experiences in Formerly Men's Colleges and Universities, 1950–2000.*, edited by Leslie Miller-Bernal and Susan L. Poulson, 3–21. Nashville, TN: Vanderbilt University Press, 2004.

Newman, Caroline. "Former Student Council President Reflects on 'May Days,' His Historic Election." *UVA Today*, May 7, 2019. https://news.virginia.edu/content/former-student-council-president-reflects-may-days-his-historic-election.

Newman, Caroline. "New Portraits, Markers Honor Important Stories and Figures in UVA History." *UVA Today*, February 16, 2022. https://news.virginia.edu/content/new-portraits-markers-honor-important-stories-and-figures-uva-history.

"1982: The Rise and Fall of Easters." *Virginia Magazine*, Spring 2011. https://uvamagazine.org/articles/1982_the_rise_and_fall_of_easters.

Office of University Development and Public Affairs. "Lawn Resident Directory, 1895–1995." 1996.

O'Shaunessey, Andrew J. *The Illimitable Freedom of the Human Mind: Thomas Jefferson's Idea of a University*. Charlottesville: University of Virginia Press, 2021.

Owen, Jan Gaylord. "Shannon's University: A History of the University of Virginia, 1959 to 1974." Ph.D. diss., Columbia University, 1993.

Perez, Caroline Criado. *Invisible Women: Data Bias in a World Designed for Men*. New York: Abrams Press, 2019.

Peril, Lynn. *College Girls: Bluestockings, Sex Kittens, and Coeds, Then and Now.* New York: W. W. Norton, 2006.

Perkins, Anne Gardiner. *Yale Needs Women: How the First Group of Girls Rewrote the Rules of an Ivy League Giant.* Naperville, IL: Sourcebooks, 2019.

Powers, Samantha. *The Education of an Idealist: A Memoir.* New York: Day Street Books, William Morrow, 2019.

Quinlan, Casey. "The Rolling Stone Story Had a Lasting Effect on the UVA Campus." *Think Progress*, November 1, 2016.

"Rector and Visitors of the University of Virginia." *Envision*, Fall 2022, 46–47.

Rice, Andrew. "Anatomy of a Campus Coup." *New York Times Magazine*, September 11, 2012.

Robertson, Louise Lilley. "Modest Pioneers: A Study of a Sample of the First-Female Class at the University of Virginia, 1970–1974." Ph.D. diss., College of William and Mary, 1986.

Savage, Barbara D. "Envisioning . . ." Parks-King lecture, Yale University, February 2, 2021.

Savage, Barbara D. "A Moment of Progressive Religious Revival." Berkley Forum, April 8, 2021.

Schlechty, Phillip C. "On the Frontier of School Reform with Trailblazers, Pioneers, and Settlers." *Journal of Staff Development* 14, no. 4 (Fall 1993): 46–51.

Shotton, Betty. "The Simple Things Said It All." *Virginia Magazine*, Fall 2011.

Smolla, Rodney A. *Confessions of a Free Speech Lawyer: Charlottesville and the Politics of Hate.* Ithaca, NY: Cornell University Press, 2020.

Solomon, Barbara Miller. *In the Company of Educated Women: A History of Women and Higher Education in America.* New Haven, CT: Yale University Press, 1985.

Steinem, Gloria. *Outrageous Acts and Everyday Rebellions.* New York: Open Road Integrated Media, 1995.

Taylor, Zari. "White Supremacy at Jefferson's University." *Inside Higher Ed*, August 10, 2018.

Tennille, Alaric. "Summer 1970, The University of Virginia Opens to Women in the Fall." In *Southern Women's Review*, February 2015.

Tough, Paul. *The Years That Matter Most: How College Makes or Breaks Us.* Boston: Houghton Mifflin Harcourt, 2019.

"Undermined by a Thousand Cuts." *Smith Alumnae Quarterly*, Spring 2018. https://www.smith.edu/news-events/news/undermined-thousand-cuts.

Unite the Right: An Exhibition in Special Collections. Alderman Library, University of Virginia, 2022.

"The UVA Lingo: Wahoos, Lawnies and Grounds." University of Virginia, May 1, 2015. YouTube. https://www.youtube.com/watch?v=4Yer9v22BJE.

White, Jeff. "'Accidental Athlete' Helped Lead the Way for Women, Black Students in Early '70s." *UVA Today*, March 17, 2022. https://news.virginia.edu/content/accidental-athlete-helped-lead-way-women-black-students-early-70s.

Willis, Judy. "Recurring Final Exam Dream?" *Psychology Today*, September 7, 2009. https://www.psychologytoday.com/ca/blog/radical-teaching/200909/recurring-final-exam-dream.

Yovanovitch, Marie. *Lessons from the Edge: A Memoir.* New York: HarperCollins, 2022.

First-Person Accounts

The following in-person, phone, and online interviews, conversations, and other communications took place 2019–24.

*entered UVA September 1970
**entered UVA September 1971 as second-year and graduated with class of 1974

George Allen**
Spindrift Beck Al Swaidi*
Wyatt Andrews*
Anonymous (multiple)*
Tom Bagby
Sharon Young Bailey*
Karen Brainard*
Margaret Ann (Ann) Brown*
Carolyn Welch Brumbaugh*
Michele Burpeau-Di Gregorio*
Cecilia Cain
John Casteen
Wayne Cozart
Liz Crowder
Leo Damrosch*
Giovana de Oliveira
Deborah (Debby) Denno*
Mary McKeone Ellmore*
Patty Kyle Epps*
Ken Elzinga
Ernest (Ernie) Ern
Petie Ern
Nancy Forbes*
Lawrence (Larry) Gerry
William (Bill) Gerry
Annette Gibbs
Brenda Weatherford Hagan*
Janet Palmer Hamel*
Jess Hamilton
Mavis Hetherington
Dale Miller Hill*
Susan Tyler Hitchcock
Elizabeth Gress Muenster Hunt*
Carolyn Hurlburt*
Alison Ingram*
Catherine (Katie) Kellett*
Susan (Susie) Clements Kiely*
Diane Kirchner Knetzger*
Phyllis Leffler
Patricia (Pat) Gritis Lessard*
Mary Bland Love*
Dick Lynch
Barbara M. Golden Lynn*
Kevin Mannix
Susanna Chiocca Mannix*
Karen Wester Marcus
Michele Martin
Kathleen McGinn*
Annette Jorgensen McKeag*
Robert (Bob) McKeag*
Elizabeth (Liz) McLeod*
Frances Dickinson (Dickie) McMullan*
Scott McWalter*
Paulette Jones Morant*
Abby Palko
Barry Parkhill
Holly Peters*
Dennis Phelan*
Christopher (Chris) Purcell*
Claudia Russell*
Larry Sabato*
Barbara Savage*
Mary Joy Scala
Virginia (Ginger) Scott
Eleanor Shannon
Betty Shotton*
Karen Skole*
Laura Wilson Small*
Carolyn Joyner Smith*
Frances Carter Stephens*
Anne Gibson Tausch*
Alarie Tennille*
Susan Byers Tribble*
Mary Payne VanderWall*
Nancy Westcott*
Margaret Combs Wales*

Rebecca (Bek) Sorrells Wheeler*
Barbara (Barb) Wilkinson*
Barbara Willette*

Oral Histories

Casteen, John Thomas. RG-26/183, University Archives, Albert and Shirley Small Special Collections Library, University of Virginia, Charlottesville, 1993.

Ern, Ernest H. RG-26/168, University Archives, Albert and Shirley Small Special Collections Library, University of Virginia, Charlottesville, 1975.

Ern, Ernest H. RG-26/230, University Archives, Albert and Shirley Small Special Collections Library, University of Virginia, Charlottesville, 1998.

Gibbs, Annette. RG-26/198, University Archives, Albert and Shirley Small Special Collections Library, University of Virginia, Charlottesville, 1991.

Hereford, Frank L., Jr. RG-26/181, University Archives, Albert and Shirley Small Special Collections Library, University of Virginia, Charlottesville, 1993.

Runk, B. F. D. RG-26/2, University Archives, Albert and Shirley Small Special Collections Library, University of Virginia, Charlottesville, 1972.

Woody, T. Braxton. RG-26/207, University Archives, Albert and Shirley Small Special Collections Library, University of Virginia, Charlottesville, 1973.

Woody, Thaddeus B. RG-26/6, University Archives, Albert and Shirley Small Special Collections Library, University of Virginia, Charlottesville, 1972.

INDEX

Italicized page numbers refer to illustrations.

abortion, 76, 120, 121, 157, 172
Accidental Athlete (film), 140
ACLU. *See* American Civil Liberties Union
African American students: admission and recruitment of, 8, 60–61; Black Alumni Weekends, 141; Black Student Alliance, 105–6, *106*, 119, 140–41; civil rights movement and, 12, 15, 16, 142, 144; desegregation and, 10, 16, 106, 142; fraternities and sororities for, 105, 111, 113; as percentage of UVA students, 163–64; racism and, 12, 25, 57, 67, 173–74; university housing for, 39–40; women in class of 1974, 6, 56–58, 60–61, 75, 85, 105–6, 139–45
Albright, Madeleine, 175
alcohol use, 78–79, 92–93, 97, 123, 125, 173
Alderman, Edwin A., 24, 126
Aldrin, Buzz, 12
Allen, George, 126, 170
Al Swaidi, Spindrift Beck, 117
Alumni Association, 3, 56, 96, 163, 164, 168
American Civil Liberties Union (ACLU), xii, 43, 44, 47, 49, 51–52, 130, 168
Anderson, Nancy, 168
Andrews, Wyatt, 56, 60, 165
anti-feminist movement, 15
anti-Vietnam War protests, 13, 15–16, 43, 44, 66, 142

Apprey, Maurice, 8
Armstrong, Neil, 12
athletics. *See* sports programs

Bagby, Tom, 101–2, 169
Bailey, Sharon Young, 85–86
Banks, Patricia, 118
basketball, 52, 79, 106, 108–9, 140
BBTOU (Bring Back the Old U) buttons, 11, 83, 102
Berkley, Francis L., Jr., 32
bias. *See* racism; sexism
Biden, Joe, 135, 161
birth control. *See* contraception
Black Alumni Weekends, 141
Black Student Alliance (BSA), 105–6, *106*, 119, 140–41
Black students. *See* African American students
Blum, Jerome, 18
Board of Visitors (BOV): coeducation accepted by, 15, 49, 51–54, 66, 72; coeducation studies and, 20, 26–28, 38–39, 41; daughters of faculty members admitted by, 25; growth goals for UVA set by, 62; on withdrawal of examination rights for women, 23–24
Brainard, Karen, 73, 114
Brewster, Kingman, Jr., 17

{201}

202 INDEX

Bring Back the Old U (BBTOU) buttons, 11, 83, 102
Brodie, Laura, 62–63
Brown, Margaret Ann, 60, 118
Brown v. Board of Education (1954), 10, 16, 52
Brumbaugh, Carolyn Welch, 73, 163
BSA (Black Student Alliance), 105–6, 106, 119, 140–41
Burpeau-Di Gregorio, Michele, 83–85
Burton, Beverly Agee, 56–58

Cain, Ceci, 153–54
campus. *See* Grounds (campus)
Canevari, Robert, 77
Casteen, John, 6, 111–12, 169
Cavalier Daily (student newspaper): on Black women enrollees for class of 1974, 60–61; "By God, I Think They're Here to Stay," 9, 9–10; "Coed Admittance to College Forced by Court Injunction," 130; demographic and enrollment information in, 6; on drug use concerns of Canevari, 77; "Feminine Attitudes," 65–66; on Honor Code violations, 78; on inferiority of Mary Washington College, 38; on Jefferson Society, 107; Love as first female business manager of, 118; on Virginia Scott, 130–31, 131; "Security Seminar Advises Women in Proper Means of Self Defense," 125; on sexual assault, 123, 124; on student support for coeducation, 26, 27; on Transition Committee, 61; "Va. Gentlewomen Meet a Man's World," 94; "Whitney Sees Gain for Men, Women in Co-Education," 27; on women's arrival to Grounds, 100
Chandler, Devin, 7–8
Cherry, Ralph, 40, 61
Churchill, Winston, 162
Civil Rights Act of 1964, 16, 25, 26, 28, 119
civil rights movement, 12, 15, 16, 142, 144
class of 1974: convocation and reception for, 75–76; enrollment statistics for, 72; Final Exercises for, 126–27; grade point averages among, 84; Honor Code contract signed by, 78; orientation for, 10, 34, 65, 75–77, 80, 87, 100, 124; physicals required for, 80; registration at Memorial Gym, 79; Shannon's welcome letter to, 75–76, 87. *See also* women in class of 1974
Clinton, Bill, 135
clothing styles, 91–92, 125
coed, origins and use of term, 18
coeducation: alumni opinions on, 11–12, 17, 20, 24, 33–34, 36, 38, 45, 62; court-mandated plans for, 6, 51; faculty opinions on, 20, 23–24, 34–36, 39–42, 46, 63, 83–86, 114; Hereford Committee on, 50; history of debates on, xi, 16, 23; Ivy League schools and, xi, 15–20, 25; male advocacy for, 16, 17, 20, 169–70; military academies and, xi, 12, 15, 19, 21, 62–63; plaque in commemoration of, 132, 168; quota system for admittance of women, 49, 50, 120; school culture and, xii, 17–18, 156; sexist responses to, 11–12; social changes impacting, 15, 16, 170–71; student opinions on, 11, 17, 20, 24, 26, 36–37, 43–44, 83; studies on desirability and feasibility of, 20, 26–39, 41, 50; Woody Committee on, 12, 28–38. *See also* women in class of 1974
COFU (Committee on the Future of the University), 26, 27, 41, 49
College of Arts and Sciences: academic quality growth due to coeducation, 84; African American students admitted to, 60–61; coeducation studies for, 20, 27–35, 40; court mandate for admittance of women to, 52; Echols scholars within, 100, 133; fiftieth anniversary of women's admission to, 56; lawsuit against denial of admissions on basis of sex, 47, 130–32; Whitney's report on women's equal access to, 41. *See also* women in class of 1974
Committee on the Future of the University (COFU), 26, 27, 41, 49

Confederate flag, 119, 141
contraception, 76, 96, 121–22
coordinate colleges, 16, 23–25, 126
Corks and Curls (yearbook), 6, 111, 138
Cornell University, 37
Coughlin, Anne, 169
Counselors Committee on Human Sexuality, 121, 122
Couric, Katie, 91
COVID-19 pandemic, 7, 135, 151, 175
Cozart, Wayne, 170
Croushore, James H., 29–33
Curtis, Tami Lynn, 38

Dabney, H. S., 87
Dabney, Virginius, 20, 92, 105, 163, 171
Daily Progress (Charlottesville newspaper), 6, 87–88, *88–89*
Damrosch, Leo, 63, 65
date rape. *See* sexual assault
Davie, Sharon, 126, 152
Davis, Harrison, 106
Davis, Lanny, 17
Davis, Lavel, Jr., 7–8
dean of women, 27, 39–43, 56, 67, 130
Denno, Deborah (Debby), 160
de Oliveira, Giovana, 58, 161, 169
desegregation, 10, 16, 106, 142
discrimination. *See* racism; sexism
"Dixie" (song), 119
Dobbs v. Jackson Women's Health Organization (2022), 120, 172
dorm counselors. *See* resident advisors (RAs)
dormitories: on Alderman Road, 71, 74, 75, 81, 90, 94; Courtenay, 71; drug raids in, 77; Dunglison, 71; Fitzhugh, 71; Lile, 78; Mary Munford, 39; Maupin, 72, 78, 94, *108*; on McCormick Road, 71, 75; parietal hours in, 74, 90; parties in, 78, 91, 93; roommate relationships in, 88–91; safety concerns for women in, 97–98; sister suites in, 76; Tuttle, 90, 94; Watson, 133; Webb, 10, 90, 99; Whitney on, 67–68

dorm talks, 76–78, 121–22, 125
drug use, 76–79, 91, 93
Drummond, Al, 106
Duckworth, Angela, 59
Dylan, Bob, 12

Easters Weekend, 33, 92
education: coordinate colleges, 16, 23–25, 126; desegregation in, 10, 16, 142; graduate and professional schools, 16, 23–24, 27, 35, 37, 40, 45, 56, 116, 130; Ivy League, 15–20, 25, 55, 156, 161; military academies, 12, 15, 19, 21, 62–63; Socratic teaching style, 86. *See also* coeducation; *specific institutions*
Ellmore, Mary McKeone, 80
Elzinga, Ken, 84, 86
Equal Protection Clause (Fourteenth Amendment), 49
Equal Rights Amendment (ERA), 15, 119, 146, 171
Ern, Ernest (Ernie): admissions seminar attended by, 18–19; on anti-coeducation sentiment, 111–12; on attrition rate for women in class of 1974, 156; on benefits of coeducation, 169; class of 1974 enrollees and, 53, 54, 60, 161–62, 164; enrollment reports by, 7, 54, 70, 72, 101, 168; interview with Virginia Scott, 44, 130; on Shannon's support for coeducation, 45
Ern, Petie, 58, 167
Everson, Kevin Jerome, 140

feminism, 15, 25, 36, 59, 145–46
field hockey, 108, *109*, 139–40
First Amendment, 49, 119
Flint, Hunter, 138
football, 76, 91, 93, 106, 110, 119, 141
Forbes, Nancy, 65, 75
Ford, Christine Blasey, 172
Fourteenth Amendment, 49, 120
fraternities, 77, 92–99, 103–4, 110–12, *111*, 119, 144, 173
Funkhouser, Laura, 94

Gard, Richard, 45, 168
Gay, Thomas B., 38
gay persons. *See* LGBTQ persons
Gay Student Alliance, 122
gender issues: barriers related to, 115, 117, 170; gender-blind admissions process, 51; gendered language, 87; politics and, 162–63, 173. *See also* men; sexism; women
Gerry, Lawrence (Larry), 13, 52, 59, 67, 81–82, 97, 127
Gibbs, Annette: on attrition rate for women in class of 1974, 156; on daughters of alumni attending UVA, 63; on faculty resistance to coeducation, 84–85; on female students as "women" not "girls," 125; on grade point averages among class of 1974, 84; on lack of activities for women at UVA, 96; on lighting and safety issues for women, 68, 98, 125; on male student reactions to arrival of women, 74; on resident advisor program, 121; on selection criteria for women in class of 1974, 36, 59; on Shannon's "let things evolve" philosophy, 100; on sorority interest in establishing chapters at UVA, 113; on sports programs for women, 102–3; on women living on the Lawn, 117–18
Ginsberg, Ruth Bader, 21
glass ceilings, 115
"Good Old Song, The" (fight song), 173
Goodrich, Cynthia, 117, 129
Greek life: for African American students, 105, 111, 113; fraternities, 77, 92–99, 103–4, 110–12, *111*, 119, 144, 173; sororities, 68, 91, 96, 104–5, 111–13, 139, 159
Grimwood, Steve, 9–10
grit, 58–59, 161, 175, 179
Grounds (campus): description of, 3–4, 22–23; drug and alcohol use on, 76–79, 91–93, 173; fiftieth anniversary of class of 1974's arrival on, 2–3, 56, 164, 168; inscription on gates to, 87; lighting on, 41, 42, 68, 81, 98, 125, 153; Memorial to Enslaved Laborers on, 174; navigation challenges, 80–82; Newcomb Hall, 71, *71*, 79, 87, 95, 99, 103; petition to ban Confederate flag from, 119; Rotunda, 22–23, 43, 66, 69–70, 139, 159, 174; safety concerns for women on, 41–42, 68, 81, 98, 125, 153; sexual assault on, 41, 98, 123, 173; shootings on (2022), 7–8; student housing shortage on, 72, 103, 104; underground tunnel network, 138. *See also* dormitories; Lawn
Gwathmey, Roberta Hollingsworth, 39, 40

Hagan, Brenda Weatherford, 157
Hamel, Janet Palmer, 118
Hammond, Lewis H., 28, 29
harassment, sexual, 123
Harold, Claudrena, 140
Harvard University, 19, 35
health services, 76, 121, 122
Hereford, Frank L., Jr., 38–39, 49, 50
Hereford Committee, 50
Hetherington, Mavis, 115
Hill, Dale Miller, 164
Hirschkop, Philip J., 43, 47
Hitchcock, Susan Tyler, 115
Homecomings, 76, 92–94
homosexuality. *See* LGBTQ persons
Honor Code, 34, 77–78, 86–87, 123, 153
Honor Committee, 36, 37, 78, 101, 138, 173
housing. *See* student housing
Huey, Mary Ann, 96
Hunt, Elizabeth Gress Muenster, 85, 95
Hurlburt, Carolyn, 114

Ihle, Elizabeth, 23, 113
Ingram, Alison, 104, 117
Ivy League schools, 15–20, 25, 55, 156, 161. *See also specific institutions*

Jackson, Ketanji Brown, 161
Jaffe, Elmer O., 10
Jaffe, Nancy, 168
Janus (Roman god of doors and transitions), 151

Jefferson, Thomas, 8, 20, 22–24, 63, 92, 136, 165
Jefferson Society, 106–8, *107*, 118, 133–34
Johnson, Martese, 173

Kasey, Gloria, 118
Kavanaugh, Brett, 172
Keene, Bill, 170
Keller, Suzanne, 156–57
Kellett, Catherine (Katie), 158
Kelly, Barbara, 103, 108
Kennedy, Joan, 56, 58, 114
Kent State University shootings (1970), 66–67
Kiely, Susan (Susie) Clements, 55
Kirstein, Jo Anne, 38, 168
Klein, Albert R., 29–32
Knetzger, Diane Kirchner, 73, 155

Land, Stanley, 106
Lawn: architectural beauty of, 98; description of, 4, 22; female residents of, 117–18, *118*, 121, 129, 137; Final Exercises on, 126–27; lighting issues, 118; surveys regarding living on, 6
League of Women Voters, 16
Leffler, Phyllis, 6, 24, 96
Lerner, Vivian, 140
Lessard, Patricia (Pat) Gritis, 90
Levine, Saul, 20
LGBTQ persons, 13, 122, 174
Love, Mary Bland, 56, 58, 118, 120
Lowe, John, xii, 44, 47, 50, 130, 164, 169
Lynch, Dick, 94
Lynn, Barbara M. Golden, 86, 106–8, *107*, 118, 132–36, *133*
Lynn, Mike, 133, 134, 136

Madison House program, 105, *105*
Malkiel, Nancy Weiss, 15, 17–18, 169–70
Mannix, Kevin, 50, 51, 61, 81, 125, 152, 169
Mannix, Susanna Chiocca, 102
Marcus, Karen Wester, 53, 90, 99
Martin, Michele, 122, 124
Martingayle, Doria, 140

Mary Washington College: *Cavalier Daily* on inferiority of, 38; transfers to UVA from, 24, 53–54, 99; as women's college for UVA, 14, 24–25, 28, 35, 53; Woody Committee representatives from, 29–33
Maxine Platzer Lynn Women's Center, 3, 122, 126, 152–53, 163
May Day Strike (1970), 44, *44*, 61, 126, 170
Mayer, E. A., 6, 113
McGinn, Kathleen, 75–76, 158
McKeag, Annette Jorgensen, 114
McKeag, Robert (Bob), 99
McLeod, Liz, 82, 127, 158, *171*
McMullan, Frances Dickinson (Dickie), 75, 113, 136–39, *137*
McWalter, Scott, 99
Meacham, Jon, 63
Memorial to Enslaved Laborers, 174
men: chauvinism of, 10, 66; coeducation advocacy by, 16, 17, 20, 169–70; fraternities for, 77, 92–99, 103–4, 110–12, *111*, 119, 144, 173; patriarchy and, 19, 22, 63, 65; rolling tradition and, 75, 96–97; sports programs for, 106, 108–9; student reactions to arrival of women, 73–75, 83, 101–2; Virginia Gentleman tradition, 3, 20, 22, 78, 87, 112, 169. *See also* gender issues
Merhige, Robert R., Jr., 49
Merritt, Kent, 106
microaggressions, 123
military academies, 12, 15, 19, 21, 62–63
Minor, C. Venable, 28–29
Moll, Richard, 25
Morant, Blake, 141
Morant, Paulette Jones, 56, 119, 139–42, *140*
Moyer, Mary, 118

Newcomb Hall, 71, *71*, 79, 87, 95, 99, 103
NOW (National Organization for Women), 146, 172

Office of Institutional Analysis, 60, 101
Owen, Jan Gaylord, 103, 170

Parkhill, Barry, 97, 109, 169
party schools, 92–93
patriarchy, 19, 22, 63, 65
Peril, Lynn, 36
Perkins, Anne Gardiner, 16–17
Perry, D'Sean, 7–8
Peters, Holly, 116–17
Phelan, Dennis, 96
physical education, 80, 108
Poe, Edgar Allan, 55
Power, Samantha, 5
pregnancies, 76, 120, 124
prejudice. *See* racism; sexism
Princeton University, 15–19, 25, 62, 98, 156
Purcell, Chris, 147–48

racism, 12, 25, 57, 67, 173–74
Rainey, John, 106
rape. *See* sexual assault
Raven Society, 36–37, 65
reproductive rights, 120, 171–72
resident advisors (RAs), 76–78, 90, 105, 121–22, 138
ReTold virtual summit, 3, 56, 96, 139, 142, 164
Rice University, 34
Roberts, Tomi-Ann, 152
Robertson, Louise Lilley, 6, 55, 96
Roebuck, James, 156
Roe v. Wade (1973), 120, 157, 170, 172
Rogers, Frank, 27
rolling tradition, 75, 96–97
Roseberry, Ed, 127
Rotunda, 22–23, 43, 66, 69–70, 139, 159, 174
Runk, B. F. D., 40, 45–46
Russell, Claudia, 157
Ryan, James E., 173, 174

Sabato, Larry, 5, 56, 114
safety concerns, 41–42, 68, 81, 97–98, 120–21, 125, 153
Salem, David, 27, 46
Savage, Barbara, 56, 118, 142–45, *143*, 160, 174

SCHEV (State Council of Higher Education for Virginia), 7, 54, 101, 168
Schlafly, Phyllis, 15
Schlechty, Phil, 128–29
Scott, Virginia A. (Ginger), xii, 44, 50, 129–32, *131*, 153, 168
sexism: of alumni, 11–12; in hiring practices, 134–35; institutionalized, 51, 171; lawsuit against UVA for, 47, 130–32; of male classmates, 11, 83; of male professors, 18, 42, 114; pay inequality and, 160; Woody Committee on, 38
sexual assault, 41, 98, 121–25, 153, 173
sexual harassment, 123
sexual minorities. *See* LGBTQ persons
Shannon, Edgar F., Jr.: on banning of Confederate flag, 119, 141; coeducation supported by, 27, 45–47, 152, 169; commencement speech for class of 1974, 126; growth goals for UVA set by, 62; on lawsuit against UVA, 45, 51–52; letters to and from Klein and Croushore, 30–33; "let things evolve" philosophy of, 100; library named for, 46, 153; reception held at home of, 76; student demands presented to, 43–44; welcome letter to class of 1974, 75–76, 87; wife and daughters of, 45–47, *46;* Woody Committee and, 28–33, 37, 38, 45
Shannon, Eleanor, 46–47
Shotton, Betty, 157
sister schools. *See* coordinate colleges
Skole, Karen, 162
Small, Laura Wilson, 80–81, 123
Smith, Carolyn Joyner, 116
Smolla, Rodney A., 174
Socratic teaching style, 86
Solomon, Barbara Miller, 19
sororities, 68, 91, 96, 104–5, 111–13, 139, 159
Special Committee on the Admission of Women to the College (Woody Committee), 12, 28–38
sports programs: club sports, 96, 103, 108, 139, 140; coed, 110, 138; desegregation

of, 106; intercollegiate, 108, *109*, 139–40; intramurals, 79, 96, 108; men's, 106, 108–9; women's, 102–3, 108, *109*, 119, 139–40. *See also specific sports*

Stanford University, 34–35

State Council of Higher Education for Virginia (SCHEV), 7, 54, 101, 168

State Female Teachers College at Fredericksburg. *See* Mary Washington College

Student Council: buses operated by, 81; coeducation supported by, 20; on equal admission of women, 50; presidents of, 5, 153–54, 156; refusal to file amicus brief, 50; social events sponsored by, 79; Transition Committee proposed by, 61; Women's Committee, 125; working group on coeducation, 26

student housing: for Echols scholars, 100, 133; fraternity houses, 77, 93, 99, 104, 112, 119; on the Lawn, 4, 6, 22, 117–18, *118*, 129, 137; off-Grounds, 77, 103–4, 121; shortage in, 72, 103–5, 121; sorority houses, 104. *See also* dormitories

Sullivan, Teresa A., 84, 153, 173

Sweet Briar College, 76

swimming requirement, 80

Tate, Vernie Merze, 145

Tausch, Anne, 83

Tennille, Alarie, *147;* on clothing styles, 91; feminism and, 145–46; "Home Coming," 149–50; path to UVA, 146–47; on pay inequality, 160; on safety concerns, 120–21; "She Doesn't Have to Call Me Bitch," 146; "Summer 1970, The University of Virginia Opens to Women in the Fall," 70–71; "Taking Forever One Day at a Time," 148–49

theater department, 114, *115*

Title IX legislation, 119–20, 139, 170

Tough, Paul, 2

transfer students, 23–24, 51, 53–54, 68, 72, 99, 102

Transition Committee, 53, 61

Tribble, Susan Byers, 73

Trudeau, Garry, 126

Trump, Donald, 172

Turner, Ulysses (Jim) Grant, 122

United States Capitol insurrection (2021), 174

United States National Student Association, 38, 47

Unite the Right rally (Charlottesville, 2017), 174

University of Virginia (UVA): administrators in 1970, *64*, 65; Alumni Association, 3, 56, 96, 163, 164, 168; clothing worn by students at, 91–92, 125; Committee on the Future of the University, 26, 27, 41, 49; *Corks and Curls* (yearbook), 6, 111, 138; dean of women at, 27, 39–43, 56, 67, 130; fight songs at, 112, 173; gender-blind admissions process at, 51; graduate and professional schools, 23–24, 27, 35, 37, 40, 45, 56, 116, 130; growth plan for, 61–63, 103, 170; health services for students, 76, 121, 122; Honor Code at, 34, 77–78, 86–87, 123, 153; language and terminology used by students, 3, 73, 77; as last public university to coeducate, 12, 19; lawsuit filed against, 15, 41, 43–44, 47–52, *48*, 130–32, 168; Maxine Platzer Lynn Women's Center, 3, 122, 126, 152–53, 163; May Day Strike at (1970), 44, *44*, 61, 126, 170; Office of Institutional Research and Analytics, 60, 101; patriarchal culture at, 22, 63, 65; relationship with Ivy League schools, 18–19, 25; reputation of, 26, 38, 55, 92–93, 172–74; School of Education, 23, 40, 61, 63, 72, 86, 116, 129; School of Nursing, 23, 63, 65, 72, 86, 116, *116;* sexual assault at, 41, 98, 121–25, 173; Transition Committee, 53, 61; tuition costs for, 55; as UNESCO World Heritage site, 23; University Guides program, 153, *154;* Virginia Gentleman tradition at, 3, 20, 22, 78, 87, 112, 169; *Virginia Magazine*, 3, 61, 157;

University of Virginia (UVA) (*continued*)
Women's Leadership Council, 152; women's studies program at, 125–26, 152. *See also* Board of Visitors; *Cavalier Daily;* class of 1974; coeducation; College of Arts and Sciences; Greek life; Grounds; sports programs; Student Council
UVA Today (website), 130, 139

VanderWall, Mary Payne, 82
Vietnam War, 12–13, 15–16, 43, *44*, 66–67, 142, 159, 170
Violence Against Women Act, 171
Virginia Council on Human Relations (VCHR), 37
Virginia Gentleman tradition, 3, 20, 22, 78, 87, 112, 169
Virginia Higher Education Study Commission, 25
Virginia Magazine, 3, 61, 157
Virginia Military Institute (VMI), 15, 21, 62–63

water polo, *110*, 138
Westcott, Nancy, 56
Wheeler, Rebecca (Bek) Sorrells, 9, 10, 83
White, Jeff, 139
Whitebread, Charles, 100, 133
Whitney, Mary: on coeducation, 39–43; as dean of women, 27, 39–43, 56, 67, 130; death and obituary of, 43; on dorm assignments, 67–68; end-of-year report by (1969), 40–44; on lighting and safety issues for women, 41, 42, 98; recruitment of transfer students, 53, 68; resignation of from UVA, 41–43; role in lawsuit against UVA, 43, 47, 130; on sororities, 68, 113; "Women and the University," 40
Wilkinson, Barbara, 158
Willette, Barbara, 95
Williams, Carla, 132, 153
Williams, D. Alan, 40, 43, 68, 113
women: abortion and, 76, 120, 121, 157, 172; contraception for, 76, 96, 121–22; coordinate colleges for, 16, 23–25, 126; feminism and, 15, 25, 36, 59, 145–46; glass ceilings for, 115; in graduate and professional schools, 16, 23–24, 27, 35, 37, 40, 45, 56, 116, 130; health services for, 76, 121, 122; labor force participation by, 4; physical education offerings for, 80, 108; pregnancies, 76, 120, 124; quota system for admittance of, 49, 50, 120; Raven Society and, 65; reproductive rights for, 120, 171–72; safety concerns for, 41–42, 68, 81, 97–98, 120–21, 125, 153; sexual assault of, 41, 98, 121–25, 153, 173; sexual harassment of, 123; sororities for, 68, 91, 96, 104–5, 111–13, 139, 159; sports programs for, 102–3, 108, *109*, 119, 139–40; as transfer students, 23–24, 51, 53–54, 68, 72, 99, 102; UVA's dean of, 27, 39–43, 47, 56, 67, 130. *See also* gender issues; sexism; women in class of 1974
women in class of 1974: academic challenges for, 82–83, 102, 115; African American, 6, 56–58, 60–61, 75, 85, 105–6, 139–45; alumni activities of, 163–64; attrition rate for, 156; clothing worn by, 91–92; as daughters of UVA alumni, 63; dorm life experiences, 88–91; faculty reactions to arrival of, 83–86; fiftieth anniversary of arrival on Grounds, 2–3, 56, 164, 168; friendships formed by, 4, 9, 99, 104, 114, 158–59; grit and perseverance of, 58–59, 138, 161, 175, 179; hands-off approach toward, 82, 100; as Lawn residents, 117–18, *118*, 121, 129, 137; legacy of, 151–54; male student reactions to arrival of, 73–75, 83, 101–2; methodology for gathering stories from, 5–7; microaggressions experienced by, 123; motivations for attending UVA, 55–58, 156; organizational involvement, *105–7*, 105–8; percentage of in-state women, 60, 70; as pioneers and trailblazers, 3, 9, 129–50, 160, 178; preparation for postgraduate life experiences, 4, 157, 159–61; selection criteria for, 36, 58–60,

161; sexism experienced by, 11–12; size of class, 3, 6–7, 13, 54, 57, 70, 129, 155; Transition Committee for, 53, 61; visits to UVA prior to school term, 68–69
Women's Center. *See* Maxine Platzer Lynn Women's Center
Women's Leadership Council, 152
Women's March (2017), 163, 171
women's rights movement, 12, 15, 16
Women's Student Association, 39

Woodstock Music and Arts Festival (1969), 13
Woody, T. Braxton, 29–30, 36, 38, 45, 91
Woody Committee (Special Committee on the Admission of Women to the College), 12, 28–38
"working on the work" strategy, 128

Yale University, 16–20, 25, 35
Yovanovitch, Marie, 18

www.ingramcontent.com/pod-product-compliance
Lightning Source LLC
Chambersburg PA
CBHW020814230426
43666CB00007B/1013